Cambridge Elements ≡

Elements in Business Strategy
edited by
J.-C. Spender
Kozminski University

EVOLUTION
OF THE AUTOMOBILE
INDUSTRY

A Capability-Architecture-Performance Approach

Takahiro Fujimoto
Waseda University

CAMBRIDGE
UNIVERSITY PRESS

Shaftesbury Road, Cambridge CB2 8EA, United Kingdom

One Liberty Plaza, 20th Floor, New York, NY 10006, USA

477 Williamstown Road, Port Melbourne, VIC 3207, Australia

314–321, 3rd Floor, Plot 3, Splendor Forum, Jasola District Centre,
New Delhi – 110025, India

103 Penang Road, #05–06/07, Visioncrest Commercial, Singapore 238467

Cambridge University Press is part of Cambridge University Press & Assessment,
a department of the University of Cambridge.

We share the University's mission to contribute to society through the pursuit of
education, learning and research at the highest international levels of excellence.

www.cambridge.org
Information on this title: www.cambridge.org/9781108468947

DOI: 10.1017/9781108658041

First published 2023

A catalogue record for this publication is available from the British Library.

ISBN 978-1-108-46894-7 Paperback
ISSN 2515-0693 (online)
ISSN 2515-0685 (print)

Evolution of the Automobile Industry

A Capability-Architecture-Performance Approach

Elements in Business Strategy

DOI: 10.1017/9781108658041
First published online: May 2023

Takahiro Fujimoto
Waseda University

Author for correspondence: Takahiro Fujimoto, fukazawa.fujimoto@gmail.com

Abstract: This Element applies the capability-architecture-performance (CAP) approach of industrial analysis to the evolution of the automobile industry and the strategies of its leading manufacturing firms between the late nineteenth century and the early twenty-first century. It regards a manufacturing site ("genba," such as a factory, development facility, etc.) and a product (and other economic artifacts, such as processes) as the two basic units of analysis. Both an industry and a firm can be seen as a collection of sites, as well as a collection of products. The CAP framework predicts that dynamic fits between the sites' organizational capabilities and the product/process architectures lead to sustainable competitive performance. Such key concepts as flows of value-carrying design information, productive/market/profit performance, design-based comparative advantage, integral/modular architectures, multiskilling, coordinative capability building, evolutionary capabilities, industry life cycle, and architectural evolution are discussed in a systematic and dynamic way.

Keywords: industrial evolution, automobile industry, competitive performance, lean manufacturing capability, integral/modular architecture

ISBNs: 9781108468947 (PB), 9781108658041 (OC)
ISSNs: 2515-0693 (online), 2515-0685 (print)

Contents

1 The Field-Based Framework of Industries and Firms

1.1 Purpose and Scope

This Element explores the evolution of the automobile industry and the strategies of its leading manufacturing firms between the late nineteenth century and the early twenty-first century. We focus on manufacturers of passenger cars, such as Daimler/Benz, Ford, GM, VW, Toyota and others, and offer additional descriptions of truck makers, parts suppliers, automobile dealers, and other service providers when necessary.

Although most of today's big businesses, striving for continued growth, have diversified into multiple sectors (Chandler, 1962), the world's leading firms in automobile manufacturing are heavily dependent on this single industry, its total being large in global terms (nearly 100 million units and $3 trillion per year in the late 2010s, possibly reaching 100 million units some time in the 2020s). We therefore regard these manufacturers as nearly single-business firms and analyze their competitive performance, strategies, and operations. Our exploration mainly covers the period between the 1880s (birth of internal combustion engines) and the 2010s, with some predictions about the 2020s and beyond.

1.2 The Field-Based Approach for Analyzing Industries and Firms

The framework adopted here to analyze a manufacturing industry and its firms is essentially evolutionary and bottom-up. More specifically, we regard a *manufacturing site* (e.g., factory, development facility) and a *product* (and other economic artifacts, such as processes) as our two basic units of analysis, from which we start our investigation of the automobile industry and firms from the bottom-up.

Both an industry and a firm can be seen as a collection of sites, as well as a collection of products. So, this Element opens with an analysis of these two. We then deal with the next question, that is, which characteristics of sites and products are worth emphasizing? In describing the manufacturing sites and products of the auto industry, we pay special attention to their *design* and *flows*. Let us now sketch out this design-flow view of manufacturing (details are discussed in later sections).

1.3 Design-Flow View of Manufacturing

In our design-flow view of industries, *design* refers to information about the relations among the functional and structural parameters of an artifact, such as a car or a computer (Simon, 1969; Suh, 1990). As Figure 1 illustrates, a product (e.g., an automobile) – as well as all its related artifacts, such as production

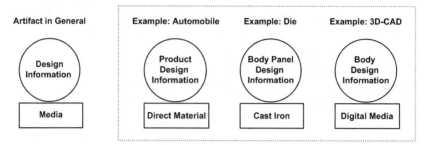

Figure 1 Productive resources as combination of value-carrying design
information and its media.

equipment, jigs and dies, standard operating procedures (SOPs), workers' skills,
numerical control programs, detailed engineering drawings, 3D-CAD models,
prototypes, design sketches, mock-ups, product specifications, and product
concept proposals – can be interpreted as a combination of design information
and its media (e.g., direct materials, digital media, drafting papers), which may
be called a productive resource (Penrose, 1959). We thus examine the automobile industry and firms starting from a design analysis of automobiles as
products.

Then, there are *flows* of design information among productive resources. The
firm's production, product development, procurement and sales activities all
involve flows of design information, eventually reaching the customers or users
of the product in question.

Design information is the source of value-added of a product, as well as its
industry. Let us assume, for instance, that a coffee mug (its design information
and medium) costs $5 and that the unit cost of its direct material (i.e., medium) is
$1 per piece. Then, its value-added is $4, which is nothing but the value of the
design information added to the mug. Thus, a product's design information is the
source of its value-added. The same logic holds true in the case of automobiles.

It follows from this analysis that the process of *manufacturing*, including
production and development, can be broadly defined as *flows of value-carrying
design information among productive resources (and ultimately to the customers)*, as indicated in Figure 2. For instance, stamping operations to manufacture
a car's body panels involve flows of design information from press dies to sheet
steel. A car's product development includes flows of incomplete design information from engineering drawings to prototypes and their test results, as well as
from body design (3D CAD) to die design (CAM) and physical dies. Hence, its
production is nothing but transfer of design information from the process (e.g.,
die) to the product (e.g., body panel).

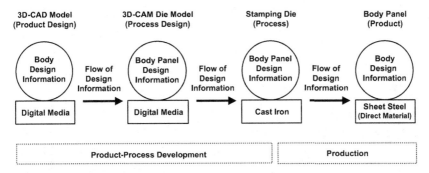

Figure 2 Manufacturing as flows of design information between productive resources (example of the automobile body).

Furthermore, to the extent that a complex artifact can be described hierarchically (Simon, 1969), we view an *industry* as total flows of value-carrying design information among *multiple hierarchies of productive resources* concerning a set of similar products, including the products' concepts, functional designs, structural designs, process designs, as well as their actual functions, structures, and processes in the physical space (Figure 3). As discussed later in the Element, these hierarchies and flows involve *transaction, competition,* and *complementation* among the productive resources of industries and firms.

Within this framework, a *manufacturing site,* or *genba* in Japanese, is nothing but a place, or a part of the industry, where value-carrying design information flows, or an organization of workers and other productive resources that govern or improve such flows. An industry can be seen as a set of manufacturing sites that deal with similar design information. Incidentally, this notion of "managing and improving flows of value-added in genba" is central to the so-called Toyota Production System (TPS).

Thus, in our bottom-up approach for analyzing the automobile industry and firms, our initial focus is on (1) the design characteristics of automobiles as products and (2) the flows of design information in automobile manufacturing sites. These two aspects are further discussed in Sections 2 and 3, respectively.

1.4 Product Architecture and Manufacturing Capability

Based on these preliminary observations, this Element proposes an *evolutionary framework* to analyze the automobile industry and firms that consists of (1) *organizational capability* of automobile manufacturing sites, (2) *product architecture* of the automobile, and (3) *competitive performance* of sites, firms and industries. These three components of our framework are all associated with

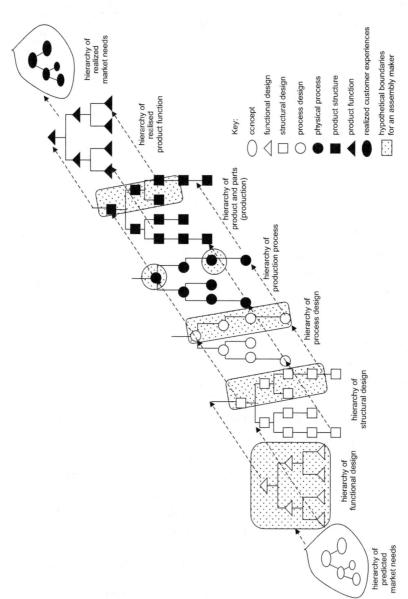

Figure 3 Industry as multiple hierarchies of design information.

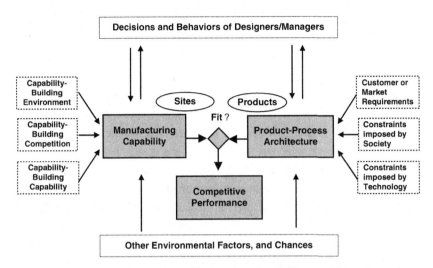

Figure 4 Design-flow view of industries: Capability, architecture, and competitiveness.

design information and its flows, which are the key concepts of our analysis (Figure 4).

Manufacturing capability: According to its definition in the routine-based view (e.g., Nelson & Winter, 1982), *manufacturing capability* is a system of organizational routines that govern the *flows* of design information to the customers both in factories and other sites. The Ford System, the modern mass-production system and TPS are prominent examples of manufacturing capabil-ities. TPS, for instance, is known as a manufacturing capability that consists of over 200 interrelated routines controlling the flows of value-carrying design information to the customers.

A certain type of manufacturing capability can evolve over time in a country characterized by a particular capability-building environment (see Figure 4). For example, the USA – a nation of immigrants – has tended to emphasize *division of labor*, or coordination-saving capability (e.g., standard-ization, modularization, specialization) whereby its firms make immediate use of incoming talent. Conversely, postwar Japan – a nation that experienced rapid economic growth and chronic labor shortage due to a lack of immigra-tion influx – had no choice but to build collaborative (coordination-rich) capability to deal with this challenge, with long-term employment and team-work involving multiskilled workers (Fujimoto, 1999, 2007a). Thus, the present framework assumes that history matters when it comes to the evolu-tion of manufacturing capability.

Product process architecture: The concept of *architecture* of a product (i.e., a tradable artifact), such as an automobile, refers to the abstract aspects of its design information, or the correspondence between the functional parameters (e.g., performance specifications) and the structural parameters (e.g., shapes of the components) of the artifact in question (Ulrich, 1995). If its function–structure relation is closer to a simple one-to-one correspondence, its architecture is said to be *modular*, while if it is closer to a complex many-to-many correspondence, its architecture is *integral*. Since design activities are essentially coordination between an artifact's functional and structural elements, we may say that modular architecture is coordination-saving, whereas integral architecture is coordination-intensive. As discussed in Section 4, highly functional automobiles – smaller cars with monocoque body structures, in particular – tend to be architecturally integral, despite the fact that auto manufacturers have put in a great deal of effort to make them more modular, so as to alleviate the design workload.

An artifact's design information has two key aspects: technology and architecture. Technology refers to concrete causal relations among structures and functions, whereas architecture describes the abstract correspondence, or mapping, among them. In order to analyze the evolution of industries and firms, we usually need to investigate both technological and architectural aspects of the products in question.

Our evolutionary framework treats a product's architecture as an endogenous (rather than exogenous) variable. As shown in Figure 4, the overall architecture of a given product category (e.g., passenger cars) can be relatively modular or integral, depending upon the nature of the functional requirements that customers expect, the constraints imposed by society and governments and the physical-technical limits inherent in the product. More specifically, a product's architecture tends toward the integral and/or closed type when such requirements are stricter, since the precise optimization of design elements is necessary to cope with more severe constraints.

By contrast, when physical constraints are less severe (e.g., weight-free digital information goods), a product's architecture tends toward the modular and open type, since engineers can more easily simplify the functional–structural connections among its design elements. Although a product's *micro architecture* may be a complex composite of modular and integral areas and layers that engineers can determine, the *macro architecture* of the whole product is affected by the market and society. Thus, there is no such thing as *intrinsic architecture* for any given product category.

Competitiveness performance: Lastly, the competitive performance of manufacturing sites, products, and firms is also defined in relation to flows of design information to the customers. The *productive performance* of manufacturing sites – such as physical productivities, production and development lead times, and manufacturing quality – measures the smoothness and accuracy of the flows of design information within such sites. A product's *market performance* refers instead to its attractiveness to potential or actual customers in terms of design, price, services, and so on.

Architecture capability fit: By using the typology of architectures and capabilities, and by applying the logic of comparative advantage found in trade theories to the locations of design activities, we have elaborated a framework of *design-based comparative advantage* (Fujimoto, 2007a, 2012). This framework, relying on the axiomatic design approach (Suh, 1990), regards product design as coordination among an artifact's functional and structural parameters. Additionally, it predicts comparative advantage in design costs when a country's endowment of a certain type of manufacturing capability fits a certain industry's architectures and other design attributes. For example, coordination-intensive (i.e., integral) products are more likely to be developed economically in a coordination-rich country (i.e., a geographical area with a strong endowment of coordinative organizational capabilities).

1.5 Organization of the Element

To sum up, our field-based bottom-up framework for analyzing the evolution of the automobile industry and firms focuses on three factors that are all related to value-carrying design information and its flows: (1) *organizational capability* of manufacturing sites, which controls flows of design information inside the factories themselves; (2) *product architecture*, which captures abstract aspects of a product's design; and (3) *competitive performance*, which measures the smoothness and attractiveness of a product's design information and its flows to the customers.

Our framework is strongly interdisciplinary, since we believe genba of industries and firms to be multifaceted economic entities. As discussed in greater detail in later sections, our capability-architecture-performance (CAP) framework integrates concepts from various fields: organizational capability from strategic management and evolutionary economics (Nelson & Winter, 1982; Grant, 1991), architecture from design theory and engineering science (Ulrich, 1995), and productive performance from industry studies, technology and operations management and neo-Ricardian economics (Womack, Jones, & Roos, 1990; Clark & Fujimoto, 1991; Holweg & Pil, 2004; Fujimoto & Shiozawa, 2011–2012).

After a preliminary discussion on the evolution and strategies of manufacturing industries and firms, we use our design-flow-based framework to analyze the market and productive *competitiveness* of the automobile industry in terms of manufacturing sites, products, and firms (Section 2).

We then introduce a design analysis of the automobile as a product. We examine the automobile's *product technology*, that is, the concrete aspects of its design, including its main components (Section 3). We also look at the automobile's *product architecture*, that is, the abstract aspects of its design, focusing in particular on its integrality and modularity (Section 4).

After that, we shift our attention to design information flows at automobile manufacturing sites. We explain the automobile's manufacturing process as design information flows, including product development, purchasing, production, and sales (Section 5). We then carry out an evolutionary analysis of the coordination-rich organizational capability of Toyota, a relatively competitive automobile firm of the late twentieth century (Section 6).

We complete our evolutionary industrial analysis by dealing with the product architecture side. We explore the automobile firms' past architectural strategies from the viewpoint of the industry life cycle (Section 7).

2 Competitive Performance of Sites, Products, and Firms

2.1 Framework: Hierarchy of Competitive Performance

2.1.1 Competitiveness as the Ability to Be Selected

In order to explore competitiveness in the automobile industry and its main causes, we first need to define and reinterpret it from our design-information perspective of manufacturing. Competitive performance can be said to measure the *goodness* of product design information and its flows.

Generally speaking, industrial competitiveness is defined as a firm's performance, giving it the ability to win in a given competition. By common-sense definition, competition is a subject's effort to be selected for a certain reward under predetermined rules and/or conditions of free choice on the part of the selectors. In other words, competition is an interaction between independent selectors and selectees. When these rules and conditions do not apply, we may call the ensuing situation collusion, coercion, conflict, and so on. In this context, *competitiveness*, or competitive performance, may be defined as *a selectee's ability to be selected by selectors* under the rule of independent choice.

2.1.2 Hierarchy of Competitive Performances

It follows from this definition of competitiveness as ability to be selected that we can classify different types of competitiveness according to what the selectee is and who the selectors are. Thus, we can conceive of at least three

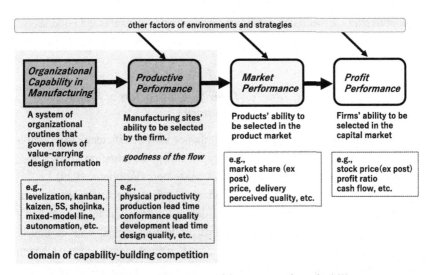

Figure 5 Capability, competitiveness, and profitability.

layers of competitive performance: (1) *profit performance*, as a firm's ability to be selected by the investors/lenders in the capital market; (2) *market perform-ance*, as a product's ability to be selected by the customers in the product market; (3) *productive performance*, as a manufacturing site's ability to be selected by the firm as its owner (Figure 5; Fujimoto, 2007a).

More specifically, *profit performance* refers to a firm's ability to be selected in the capital market (e.g., return on sales, return on assets, return on equity), or its attractiveness as a whole in the minds of the investors. The level of *profit performance* is affected by the firm's productive and market performance, as well as by other factors, such as exchange rates, business cycles, and strategic choices.

Market performance is a product's ability to be selected in the product market, or the attractiveness of the design information embodied in the product in question in the minds of the customers. The product's ex ante market performance includes price, delivery time, and perceived quality, whereas its ex post market performance is measured by its market share. We may also call market performance *surface-level competitiveness*, as it is revealed on the surface of the market that can be observed by the customers.

Productive performance, including productivity, lead times and manufactur-ing quality, measures a manufacturing site's ability to be selected as a surviving facility by the firm that owns it. Thus, a firm's manufacturing sites compete to be selected by its headquarters and top managers. Since this selection is made at a level that is not visible to the customers, we may also call it *deep-level competitiveness*. Essentially, productive performance measures the goodness of design information flows among productive resources in the manufacturing sites.

2.1.3 Quality, Cost, Time, and Flexibility as Factors of Productive Performance

The essential aspects of productive performance include efficiency (productivity and lead times) and accuracy (quality) of design information flows across productive resources and eventually to the customers (Fujimoto, 1999).

In the case of production sites (factories), physical *productivity* is the production process's efficiency in sending design information to the product's materials (i.e., media). Given the price of production inputs, such as hourly wage rates or equipment costs, higher productivity means lower *unit cost*, which may be regarded as another efficiency-related indicator when input prices are stable and uniform across sites and over time. Likewise, *production lead time*, or time elapsed between receiving the direct materials and shipping the product, is the materials' efficiency in receiving design information from the production process. *Manufacturing quality* refers to the accuracy of design information transmission from the process to the product's materials or work in process. We can also define development productivity, development lead time, and design quality in a similar way for product development processes (Clark & Fujimoto, 1991).

Flexibility is another indicator of competitive performance, which measures the stability of the aforementioned performance aspects (e.g., productivity, unit cost, lead time, quality) vis-à-vis changes in product designs, production volumes, and other manufacturing conditions. Thus, we may identify quality, cost (productivity), time (lead time), and flexibility (QCTF) as the four main factors of productive performance.

2.1.4 An Industry's Competitive Performance

We have so far discussed competitive performance at the level of firms (profit performance), products (market performance), and sites (productive performance). What about performance at the level of a country's industry?

As already mentioned, an industry is a collection of manufacturing sites or their products, but it is not necessarily a collection of firms, which can be multi-industrial and/or multinational. Accordingly, it is not relevant to aggregate firms' profit performance at the industry level. This aggregation may however be allowed as an approximation when the firms in question can be regarded as nearly single-industry firms, as is the case with most of the major automakers.

An industry's ex post *market performance*, measured by market share, can be aggregated as a country's market share in the global/local market. As for price, quality and delivery, their distribution or average levels vis-à-vis rival countries may be used as summary indicators. An industry's *productive performance* indicators, such as productivity, lead time and defect ratios, may also be captured as their distribution or average levels vis-à-vis rival countries or regions (Womack, Jones, & Roos, 1990; Clark & Fujimoto, 1991).

2.1.5 From Manufacturing Capability to Productive Performance

As shown in the left portion of Figure 5, the causal relations between manufacturing capability (i.e., the system of organizational routines that govern and improve the flows of value-carrying design information) and productive performance (i.e., the resulting goodness of such flows) are fairly straightforward (Schonberger, 1982; Monden, 1983; Womack, Jones, & Roos, 1990; Fujimoto, 1999).

As an example, let us look at the relations between Toyota/lean-style capability and productive performance. Both productivity and production lead time improve as *value-adding time ratios*, that is, the percentage of time during which design information flows from the process to the product out of the total operation time (in the former case) or lead time (in the latter case). The time when information is *not* transferred from the process to the product is made up of *muda* (waste, or unnecessary non-value-adding time) and ancillary work time (necessary non-value-adding time) in TPS (Ohno, 1978). Reducing non-value-adding time results in shortening lead times and enhancing productivities, other things being equal.

In our design-flow view of manufacturing, the following formulas always hold true, where X is daily production (e.g., 1,000 units per day in a typical car assembly plant), W is daily working hours of all workers (e.g., 10,000 person-hours if 1,250 workers work 8 hours per day), V is total daily value-sending time (e.g., 1,000 hours if 1 hour is needed per vehicle), T is production lead time in hours (e.g., 50 hours), and v is average value-receiving time per vehicle (1 hour per vehicle).

Productivity $= X/W = [X/V] \times [V/W] =$ [value-sending speed] $\times$ [value-sending density]

1/Lead Time $= 1/T = [1/v] \times [v/T] =$ [value-receiving speed] $\times$ [value-receiving density]

In this example, productivity is 0.1 vehicle per person-hours, value-sending speed is 1, value-sending density is 25%, value-receiving time is 1, and value-receiving density is 2%. These numbers approximate today's better-performing assembly plants carrying out welding, painting, and final assembly processes.

It follows from this production logic that these better-performing factories still have high ratios of non-value-adding time: 75% on the value-sending side (productivity in the operation), including workers' waiting times and walking times, and 98% on the value-receiving side (lead time in the process), including inventory times and the materials' waiting times. Hence, if one of these factories implements various manufacturing routines to reduce non-value-adding time and increase value-adding time ratios, such as Just-in-Time, autonomation (*jidoka*), multiskilling, and *kaizen* (continuous improvement), it is likely to enjoy higher productivities and shorter lead times vis-à-vis rival plants. We call the efforts of firms and sites to enhance their capabilities and productive performance *capability-building competition*, which we discuss later on.

2.2 Competitive Performance of Automobile Firms and Industries

Let us now take a brief look at the competitive performance of firms, products, and industrial sites across the world's automobile industries.

2.2.1 Profit Performance

To the extent that the world's major automobile manufacturers may be regarded as nearly single-industry firms, we may compare the profit performance of such firms.

In the mid-twentieth century, the US *Big Three* enjoyed relatively high profit ratios, due both to their domestic oligopoly and to the lack of international competition in the segment of the American-style large body-on-frame vehicles of those days. When the two oil crises of the 1970s led US market demand to shift toward smaller unit-body cars, international competition in the small car segment intensified, particularly vis-à-vis exports by Japanese manufacturers, resulting in the US automakers suffering massive losses in the early 1980s.

The US government adopted a protectionist approach by virtually restricting Japanese exports of vehicles and parts, which sparked a rush by several Japanese automakers and roughly 200 parts suppliers to build plants in the USA throughout the 1980s. Intense competition in the small car segment continued, and the US carmakers – which had historically been good at manu-facturing relatively modular vehicles with body-on-frame structures but not integral ones with monocoque bodies – were affected by decreasing profit performance.

In the 1990s, as larger body-on-frame vehicles (e.g., minivans, sports utility vehicles (SUVs), pickup trucks) regained popularity among the US baby boomers with standard households, the profit performance of American car-makers recovered. After the financial crisis of 2008, however, this profitable market collapsed, and their profit performance dropped considerably. GM went bankrupt and Chrysler was sold to the European firm FIAT.

The profit performance of European firms varied from segment to segment. While European mass producers often suffered from low or negative profits, luxury carmakers (e.g., Daimler-Benz, BMW) enjoyed higher profit ratios. Japanese manufacturers tended to depend on relatively high profit from their exports and sales in the US market, which made up for lower profits in the Japanese market, characterized by tough domestic competition. Korean firms, on the contrary, tended to rely on high profits in their oligopolistic domestic market, which made it possible for them to apply relatively low prices and successfully compete in overseas markets for many years.

With this overview in mind, let us look at the profit performance of the major automakers between the 1990s and the 2010s (Figure 6). Data regarding operating profit per sales of 13 firms in the USA, Europe, Japan, and Korea were collected and calculated. To visualize and compare long-term trends across firms and regions, different colors are allocated to different profit levels.

Here follow some observations about Figure 6. First, in most cases, the profit rates were either 0–5% or 5–10%, with a simple average of roughly 5%. There were sporadic cases of 10%+ performance, but they were short-lived, with the exception of BMW in the 2010s. Thus, compared with most ICT industries, for instance, this is a relatively low-profit-rate industry, although its profit size is large because of its sheer size. Second, most of these firms went through bad periods with negative profits in different years and for various reasons, but they always recovered from them, at least for some time. The longest slumps were experienced by the US firms during the 2000s and at other times, leading to GM's bankruptcy, but their performance somewhat improved in recent years. Third, there were some interregional performance differences. Simple averages after 2000 were 6–7% for European luxury carmakers, 5–6% for Japanese firms, 3–4% for other European automakers, and around 0% for the US ones. In the 2010s, however, profit rates tended to converge into the 5–10% range, with the Western volume producers catching up with their East Asian counterparts.

To sum up, in this century, the major automakers across the world have experienced relatively low, mostly single digit, returns on sales (ROS), with some ups and downs, but they have shown a certain amount of tenacity by recovering from their respective slumps and surviving until now, at least as semi-independent parts of the global auto industry. Interfirm ROS gaps do exist, but they are neither dramatically large nor diverging in the long run. Thus, compared with the rapidly growing ICT sector, the auto industry of this century

Firm	Home	1990	1995	2000	2001	2002	2003	2004	2005	2006	2007	2008	2009	2010	2011	2012	2013	2014	2015	2016	2017	2018
General Motors	US	-4	3.8	3.9	1.5	1.3	1.6	0.6	-8.8	-3.7	-2.4	-14.3	-20.0	3.8	3.8	19.9	3.3	1.0	3.2	5.7	5.9	7.0
Ford	US	-5.2	2.8	3.8	-5.7	-0.4	-1.1	-0.1	-2.7	-12.5	-2.8	-7.2	-2.6	4.9	4.3	3.6	3.0	-0.8	3.8	3.1	1.9	0.4
Volks Wagen	Germany	-1.7	-2.3	4.8	6.1	5.5	2.0	1.8	2.9	1.9	5.6	5.6	1.8	5.6	7.1	6.0	5.9	6.3	-1.9	3.3	6.0	5.9
Daimler Benz	Germany			4.9	6.2	5.9	5.6	3.3	-1.0	3.5	9.1	4.4	-1.2	8.7	9.0	7.-	6.2	8.0	9.5	9.1	9.4	7.8
BMW	Germany			4.7	3.2	4.9	7.8	8.0	7.0	8.4	6.9	0.7	0.8	8.0	10.7	10.2	10.4	10.8	10.0	10.3	10.9	10.1
PSA	France	9.8	1.7	4.8	5.1	5.4	4.1	4.4	3.4	2.0	2.9	1.0	-1.4	3.2	2.2	-1.0	-0.3	1.5	5.0	6.0	6.4	7.7
Renault	France	9.9	0.7	4.2	1.9	1.7	3.3	3.3	5.3	2.6	3.3	0.6	-1.2	2.8	2.6	1.8	3.0	3.9	5.2	6.4	6.5	6.3
Fiat	Italy	4.2	4.4	1.5	0.5	-1.4	-1.1	0.1	2.1	3.8	5.5	5.7	2.3	3.1	4.0	4.1	3.5	3.0	4.3	5.5	6.4	6.3
Toyota	Japan	5.1	3.3	6.1	7.5	8.0	8.8	7.8	8.1	8.6	9.3	-2.2	1.5	3.0	1.5	4.4	7.1	8.0	10.1	10.0	7.2	8.2
Nissan	Japan	2.1	0.7	4.8	7.8	10.3	10.6	9.4	9.2	7.4	7.3	-1.6	4.1	6.1	6.8	5.0	4.8	5.2	6.5	6.3	4.8	2.7
Honda	Japan	3.4	3.4	6.3	8.7	8.7	7.4	7.3	7.4	7.7	7.9	1.9	4.2	6.4	2.9	5.5	6.3	5.2	3.4	6.0	5.4	4.6
Suzuki	Japan	4.4	4.6	3.2	3.5	3.7	4.3	4.5	4.1	4.2	4.3	2.6	3.2	4.1	4.8	5.5	6.4	6.0	6.1	8.4	10.0	8.4
Hyundai	Korea		5.4	7.2	7.8	6.5	5.8	4.5	3.9	2.8	4.1	3.9	6.1	8.8	10.3	10.0	9.5	8.5	6.9	5.6	4.8	2.5

Legend: 10%- | 5-10% | 0-5% | negative

Figure 6 Profit performance – operating profit to sales ratios of major automobile manufacturers (1990~2018).

has so far had more limited growth and profitability, but it has been significantly less disrupted. Thus, those who predict that a big wave of disruptions will hit the auto industry too have to explain logically why it did not happen in the past but will happen in the future.

Let us now analyze profit performance by region in more detail. Since the late twentieth century, the profit performance of US-based firms (e.g., GM, Ford, Chrysler) has tended to depend upon the strength of the demand, within the North American market, for trucks or body-on-frame vehicles (e.g., pickup trucks, large SUVs, minivans), which are larger, heavier and architecturally more modular than monocoque-type passenger cars. Therefore, profits have generally been higher in periods when oil prices were lower and government regulations on corporate average fuel economy (CAFE) less stringent. On the contrary, the profit performance of Japanese manufacturers (e.g., Toyota, Nissan, Honda) has tended to be higher in periods when North American demand for smaller, lighter and architecturally more integral cars (mostly with monocoque bodies) was stronger, with higher oil prices and stricter CAFE regulations.

The profit performance of European carmakers (e.g., VW, Daimler, Renault, PSA, Fiat) has tended to rely on the small or luxury car markets in Europe and in non-US emerging regions, including China, where VW has been particularly strong. Being a latecomer to the US market, the Korean manufacturer Hyundai-Kia has had no choice but to diversify its profit-generating regions to Europe, emerging nations and Korea itself. Accordingly, its international profit performance is more balanced than that of other global automakers.

As for emerging regions, such as China, India, Latin America and Africa, the profitability of their automobile markets and the profit performance of local automakers are still hard to predict. Conversely, the profit performance of global automakers in these emerging markets may be similar to their performance in advanced nations: the US manufacturers are stronger in the segment of larger body-on-frame vehicles, the European firms are more competitive in small monocoque vehicles or luxury cars, while the Japanese firms are leaders in small and fuel-efficient vehicles (e.g., hybrid vehicles).

2.2.2 Market Performance

We now turn to the market shares, or ex post market performance, of firms and countries (i.e., domestic industries). We examine two types of shares (in units or revenue): (1) *sales shares* of auto manufacturers by country or region and (2) *production shares* of auto manufacturers by country or region (Figure 7: data provided by the research firm FOURIN). Note here that the difference between

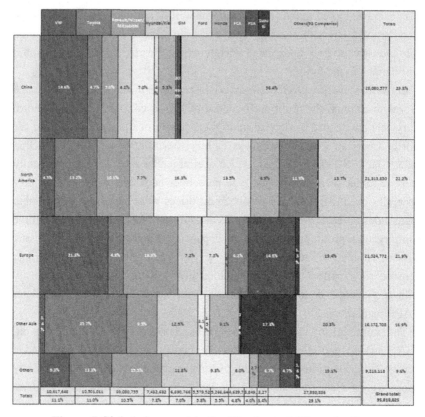

Figure 7 Global share matrix for (1) sales and (2) production.

a firm's production and sales in a country can roughly be regarded as its estimated net export/import volume in that country. Additionally, the worldwide production or sales share of a firm can be seen as its worldwide *design share*.

(1) Global Sales Share Matrix (10 largest groups)
(2) Global Production Share Matrix (10 largest groups)

Keeping these preliminary remarks in mind, let us introduce a global market share matrix arranged according to firms (horizontal axis) and countries (vertical axis), which provides a visual representation of the automobile firms' geographical patterns of market performance. The area of each box represents sales/production volume of each firm in each country.

A glance at the global market share matrices for (1) sales and (2) production in 2018 allows us to notice the following:

• As for the country axis, China has become the world's largest automobile market in recent years (its share being about 30%), followed by the USA and

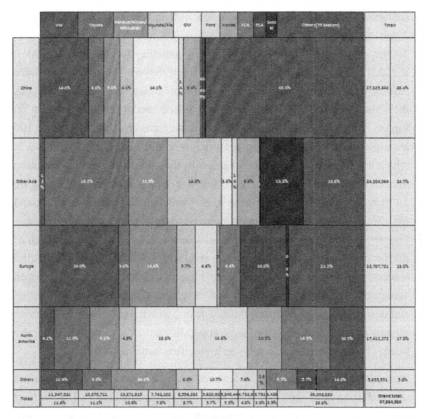

Figure 7 (cont.)

the EU (with shares of around 20% each). The Indian market has also experienced considerable growth. All told, Asia held over 50% of the production share in the world auto industry of the 2010s.

- As for the firm axis, each of the largest global firms/groups, including their subsidiaries and allies (such as VW, Toyota, GM), occupies roughly 10% of the world automobile market in terms of units. At present, Korea's Hyundai-Kia is the only global giant outside the traditional auto-making regions (i.e., North America, Western Europe and Japan). The 10 largest groups identified in these matrices (including Renault-Nissan-Mitsubishi and Fiat Chrysler Automobiles) account for about 70% of both sales and production worldwide. Incidentally, if we define a firm based on the 50% ownership rule, the 10 largest firms occupy somewhat smaller portions of the world market, that is, less than 70% in sales and less than 60% in production, respectively.

- In the late 2010s, the concentration ratio of the 10 largest groups by region was high in North America (about 90%), low in rapidly growing China (around 50%), and medium in Europe and non-Chinese Asia (including Japan, with about 80%).

- So, the world auto industry is certainly oligopolistic, but not extremely so. It is rather hard to identify the number of automakers worldwide that have sufficient development/production/sales capabilities, but certain statistics may shed some light on the matter. Indeed, according to the data in Figure 7, including commercial vehicle manufacturers, there are about 100 automakers/groups in sales and about 90 in production worldwide, many of which are Chinese domestic companies. In the mid-2010s, there were more than 20 automakers producing more than 1 million automobiles, and roughly 50 firms, including many Chinese ones, producing more than 50 thousand units (OICA: International Organization of Motor Vehicle Manufacturers).

- Overall, the matrices show the regional sales/production presence of each of the firms like a skyline on the horizontal axis, which indicates a natural tendency toward being strong in their home regions. All told, Japan-based automobile firms hold roughly 30% of the global shares of sales, production and design, followed by Europe-based firms, which indicates that these two regions tend to enjoy design-based comparative advantages in architecturally relatively integral products, such as highly functional automobiles.

Historically, Europe was the world's center of automobile manufacturing in the late nineteenth century, but the USA, with Ford and GM, secured the vast majority of the world's auto production in the early twentieth century. Then in the latter half of the twentieth century, Europe and Japan developed into the two main automobile-producing regions. In the twenty-first century, some emerging nations, including China and India, have become prominent manufacturers. These emerging nations, led by China, now control around half of the world's automobile sales and production.

2.2.3 Productive Performance

The most systematic international comparative studies on productive performance were conducted around the year 1990 (Womack, Jones, & Roos, 1990; Clark & Fujimoto, 1991; Cusumano & Nobeoka, 1998). Their key findings are reported next, along with a discussion of what happened after that period.

Physical Assembly Productivity: The International Motor Vehicle Program (IMVP) is one of the most reliable sources of information on the physical productivity of assembly factories (i.e., body welding, painting and final assembly shops) by country/region, including the USA, Europe, and Japan (Womack, Jones, & Roos, 1990). The International Motor Vehicle Program data are presented in the form of person-hours per vehicle, or the inverse of productivity, so the smaller the figure, the higher the productivity. According to the IMVP surveys, in the late 1980s the average figures were as follows: 17 in Japan, 25 in the USA, and 36 in Europe. This evidence triggered a boom in the adoption of lean production systems, which IMVP advocated as a source of Japan's competitive advantage.

During the 1990s, the gaps among average assembly productivities started to narrow, as Western firms caught up with their Japanese competitors. The IMVP survey carried out in 2000 revealed that average assembly person-hours were 12 in Japan, 17 in the USA, and 20 in Europe (Figure 8; Holweg & Pil, 2004). Thus, international capability-building competition in productivity was certainly working in this industry, also due to the benefits of lean production adopted by Western firms.

And yet, Japanese sites managed to retain their advantage by continuing to improve their capabilities. At the beginning of the twenty-first century, Japan's average assembly productivity approached 10 person-hours per vehicle according to a follow-up study by IMVP (in which the author was also involved). As Asia established itself as a center of the world's automobile production, we did a similar IMVP follow-up study there in the 2000s, still using the original measurement method of IMVP 1990 (Womack, Jones, & Roos, 1990). The results indicate that the assembly productivity of the Japanese automakers' transplants in China was, on average, around half that of their domestic plants

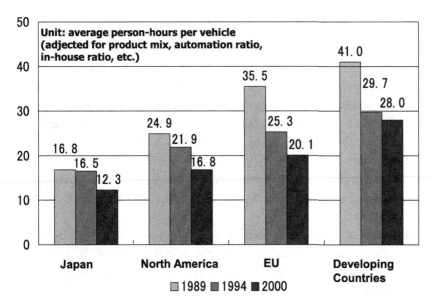

Figure 8 Average assembly productivities by region: results of International Motor Vehicle Program surveys.

in Japan. Our field surveys also suggest that the productivity of the local assembly factories of Chinese firms tended to be significantly lower than that of the abovementioned transplants. Likewise, the average productivity of the Japanese firms' transplants in India was about a fourth that of their domestic plants.

Although drastic automation and robotization relying on artificial intelligence and the Internet is currently a much-discussed topic, the assembly productivities of the world's automobile firms will progress rather incrementally. This will be partly because robotization of the welding lines was already achieved by the 1990s and partly because we predict that complete final assembly robotization will continue to be technically difficult even in the 2020s, due to its physical complexity. We will discuss this in greater detail later.

Manufacturing Quality: For what concerns the manufacturing quality of the automobiles in the US market, professional organizations, such as J.D. Power and Consumer Reports, have carried out consistent comparative studies on initial conformance qualities (e.g., the number of defects reported per vehicle in the first 90 days of operations) for many years. As the IMVP 1990 study suggested, Japanese automobile manufacturers generally maintained advantages over their US and European rivals. During the 1990s, however, the US firms, followed by their Korean competitors, started to narrow the quality gap vis-à-vis the Japanese carmakers. Thus, in manufacturing quality as well, international capability-building competition was working in this particular industry.

Production Lead Time: While IMVP and other industrial performance studies (e.g., Womack, Jones, & Roos, 1990) did not include international comparisons of production lead times, in the late 1990s the author counted the number of bodies in assembly factories, from the beginning of the welding line to the end of the final assembly line, as a proxy for their lead time. In Japan, the average number of bodies was about 1,000 throughout the whole process, including bodies in the value-adding workstations and those as buffers, whereas the most buffered plant in Europe had nearly 3,000 bodies per line. Thus, in terms of this productive performance indicator, the Japanese sites had a competitive advantage over their rivals thanks to the buffer-reducing capabilities of lean production.

Assuming a typical high-volume assembly factory with a capacity of 60 vehicles per hour (1 minute takt time), the minimum possible lead time, in case of zero downtime on the line, would be about 16 hours (1,000/60). If the factory operates on a 16-hour day with two shifts, this means that a body starting from workstation #1 of the welding line may reach the end of the assembly line by the end of the same day.

2.2.4 Product Development Performance

In the late 1980s, Clark & Fujimoto (1991) conducted an international comparative study of productive performance in product development, including development productivity, development lead times, and total product quality. The study pointed to significant advantages of Japanese development projects in terms of both productivity (measured as adjusted engineering person-hours per project) and lead time (measured as months elapsed between a new model being conceived and its market introduction).

The author and colleagues (including Christophe Midler and Kentaro Nobeoka) continued to measure the product development performance of European and Japanese projects in the 2000s and found the following: (1) Japanese projects maintained their advantages in both lead time and productivity; (2) Japanese lead time performance essentially ceased to improve; (3) in Europe, the average person-hours per project increased, probably due to increased complexity of the product and its product mix (Figure 9).

In the 2020s, however, there will be at least two significant technological changes that may affect the product development performance of global automakers. First, today's automotive product development processes are evolving into full-scale virtual engineering based on 3D-CAD models and computer-aided engineering (CAE) simulations at the level of the total vehicle. Second, today's automobiles are equipped with a huge amount of embedded software for electronic control of the vehicle and its modules, and such software, without the constraints of physical laws, leans toward a more open/modular architecture (e.g., standardized basic software and its interfaces).

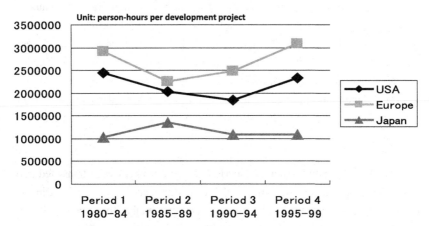

Figure 9 Average development productivities by region and period: results of the Harvard International Product Development Project.

Thus, to the extent that the leading Japanese automakers have enjoyed design-based comparative advantages in human-team-based coordination and integrative product engineering with physical prototypes (Clark & Fujimoto, 1991), the advancement of virtual engineering and on-vehicle software may reduce such advantages. On the other hand, to the extent that the Japanese firms maintain stronger coordinative capabilities, whether the prototypes are physical or virtual (Thomke & Fujimoto, 2000), they may keep on enjoying design-based comparative advantage in the era of digitization. Which scenario will come true remains to be seen in the 2020s and beyond.

2.3 Design-Based Comparative Advantage

Overall, the data and analysis of the competitive performance of sites, products, firms, and national industries suggest that, as far as productive performance is concerned, Japanese firms tended to outperform their rivals from the 1980s to the 2010s at least. In this regard, we may explore the following key issues: (1) why these Japanese productive performance advantages continued for such a long time; (2) whether the Japanese productive performance advantages were translated into advantages in market and profit performance; and (3) whether the Japanese competitive advantage will continue in the 2020s and beyond, when automobile-related technologies are predicted to change quite radically.

In order to shed light on these issues, we apply the CAP view of industries and firms presented in Section 1 (Figure 4). According to this framework, we may conclude the following:

1. Mostly for historical reasons, in the postwar period Japanese auto firms were somehow forced to accumulate coordination-rich (collaborative) manufacturing capabilities based on teamwork and a multiskilled workforce. According to the concept of design-based comparative advantage, these types of firms and sites should outperform their rivals when the product in question is coordination-intensive in its design and operation. The high-performance automobiles of the 1970s and following decades, with ever stricter constraints regarding safety, emissions, and energy efficiency, were typical examples of such coordination-intensive or architecturally integral products.

2. It is true that Japan's productive performance advantages were translated into market performance, in terms of global market shares (roughly 30% in the 2010s) and exports (around five million units between the 1980s and the 2010s), and, to a less extent, into profit performance (Toyota's profit was positive between 1950 and 2008 and remained the world's largest in the late 2010s).

Nevertheless, the process of global competition was far from one-sided. Some European carmakers (e.g., VW) competed very effectively in architectural innovations, among which was the modularization of integral vehicles. Although their competitiveness in small-integral vehicles continued to decline, US firms enjoyed competitive advantages in large modular automobiles, such as pickup trucks and SUVs, well into the 2010s. China, now the world's largest automobile market (about 30 million units as of the late 2010s), was typically dominated by foreign firms, but local manufacturers are gaining market shares, above all in relatively modular vehicles, such as trucks and body-on-frame SUVs. Thus, while Japan continues to retain its advantages in manufacturing capability and productive performance in the early twenty-first century, its rivals are competing rather effectively in architectural positioning and architectural innovations.

3. The future of competition in the automobile industry of the twenty-first century will also depend on the evolution of automobile technologies (e.g., software for electronic control, autonomous driving, electrification), product architectures (e.g., modularization), production/development technologies (e.g., virtual engineering, digital manufacturing), as well as manufacturing capability, capability-building capability, and architecture-building capability, by automobile firms across the globe, whether they are new entrants or incumbents.

The matters discussed here will be analyzed in the following sections by looking at the automobile product technologies, product architectures, automobile manufacturing as value flows, manufacturing capabilities, capability-building capabilities, and architecture-building capabilities of firms, sites, and industries.

3 Product Technology of the Automobile

3.1 Today's Automobiles

Within our field- and design-based analysis of industries and firms, which focuses on products and manufacturing sites as its first step, it is logical to start our discussion from the automobile regarded as a product. Since our framework, proposed in Section 1, views a product as a tradable artifact, or a *designed thing* with economic value (Simon, 1969), we study the automobile mainly from the point of view of its design. While our concept of design has two aspects – *technologies* and *architectures* – our main topic in this section is the product's core technologies, or the relations between structural and functional elements of the automobile and related artifacts.

3.1.1 Motor Vehicles as Fast-Moving Heavy Objects

Let us first describe today's small, high-performing and fuel-efficient passenger cars. It may be difficult to precisely say what an automobile is but, if we had to explain the concept to someone alien to it, we could give the following definition:

> *It is a heavy machine (mostly over 1 ton) with wheels (mostly 4), propelled by a certain powertrain (e.g., internal combustion engine, electric motor) and controlled mainly by a skilled operator with some automatic assistance, which can move fast (typically 20~200 km/h) and carry people or goods between any point A and point B that are connected by open roads.*

Because of their mass and speed, today's automobiles have become very complex in their mechanical and electronic design, and they are one of the most highly priced consumer goods for many of us.

3.1.2 Numerous Automobiles on Earth

Despite their high price and big size, there are numerous automobiles on earth. In the 2010s there were over 1.2 billion cars and trucks in use globally, or about one vehicle per five people, and the number is due to grow further in this century, mainly in populous emerging countries. In terms of mobility, although the average asset utilization ratio of cars is not high (roughly 5%), total trip distance is estimated to be roughly eight trillion kilometers – a figure which is expected to double by 2030. As a result of this massive usage, transportation, most of which concerns automobiles, is responsible for nearly 30% of annual energy consumption and over 20% of carbon dioxide emissions worldwide.

3.2 Basic Product Technologies of the Automobile

3.2.1 Mobility as the Automobile's Main Function

Today's highly functional automobiles are characterized by extreme complexity, with over 30,000 piece-parts and a hundred million lines of embedded software code. Even though they serve various purposes, including personal mobility, status symbol, aesthetic pleasure, and being fun to drive, for the sake of simplicity, we restrict our investigation to the mobility aspects of these artifacts. Figure 10 provides a very simplified view of the automobile and mobility, that is, its main function.

3.2.2 Main Structural Elements of the Automobile

Let us now explore the automobile's product technology. In our design-based framework, a product's technology refers to concrete causal knowledge of the artifact's structural and functional elements, given control and other environmental

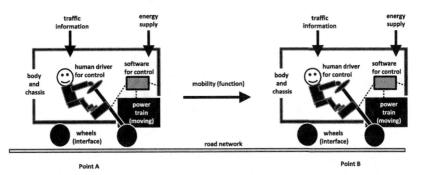

Figure 10 The automobile and mobility: a simplified model.

inputs. For example, a motor vehicle's function (mobility) is determined by its hardware structure (e.g., body, chassis, engine, steering, wheels), software for electronic control, operator (driver) for human control, and other environmental/ infrastructural factors, such as road network, energy supply (gas stations), and traffic information (traffic lights, signs, road information). In other words, our simple equation of a product's technology is as follows:

mobility as function = f (vehicle's hardware structure, software for control, operator for control, environmental and other inputs)

Note here that, in today's automotive product development, this causal relation can be verified and validated either through physical testing (e.g., measured function, physical prototype, electronic control unit (ECU), test driver, and test course) or through mathematical simulation (e.g., computed function, 3D-CAD vehicle model, embedded software, virtual driver model, and 3D digital map) or by using hybrid forms of physical and virtual means.

Figure 11 presents a model of the automobile technology that, despite being highly simplified, still looks rather complex.

The left-hand side of Figure 11 includes the major structural elements, or components, of the automobile. The 30,000 piece-parts in today's typical automobile are grouped into several main modules that are functionally rather complete: wheels, main body (chassis and upper body), powertrain (engine and transmission) and manipulators, such as steering, brakes, accelerator, and gear shifter. Their historical evolution and key functions are briefly described in Section 3.3. The right-hand side of Figure 11 shows the technical and customer functions. These functions are summarized in terms of overall economic value and socioeconomic costs of the automobile.

The arrows between the left-hand side and the right-hand side of Figure 11 represent the main causal relations among the automobile's structural and functional elements, given their control by the human driver and

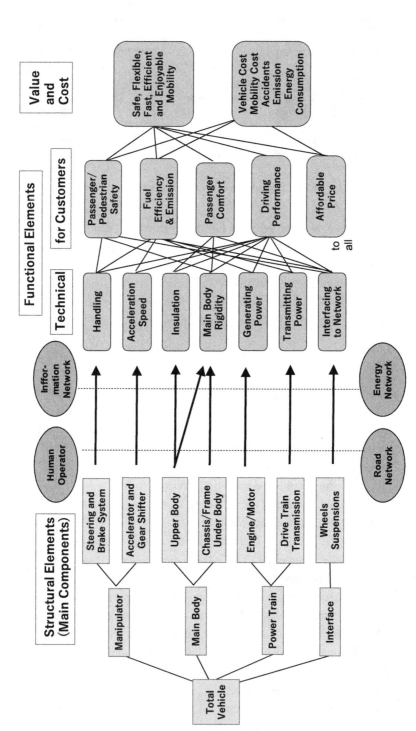

Figure 11 Simplified view of the automobile technology.

through software. Each component may perform only one function or serve multiple functions; similarly, a certain function may be affected by multiple components. We also introduce other inputs that may influence the mobility of the automobile: roads as physical network, energy supply network, and traffic information systems. As for the vehicle hardware, its four major subsystems – wheel/tire, body/chassis, powertrain, and steering/accelerator/ brake – are illustrated next.

3.3 Main Components of the Automobile

3.3.1 Wheels and Tires as Flexible Interface

The wheels, which connect the vehicle and the road, are arguably the oldest technology of the automobile. The earliest versions of the wheel include wooden rollers for building the Pyramids, wooden wheels with spokes for carriages, steel wheels for locomotives, as well as solid rubber tires with steel wire spokes for bicycles. The first steam-powered automobile by Cugnot (1769) had three wooden spoke wheels, whereas the first gasoline engine vehicle by Benz (1886) adopted bicycle-type wheels with steel spokes and solid rubber tires. The pneumatic rubber tires, first invented by Dunlop (1888) for bicycles, quickly improved in their inner structure and were integrated into the automobile by the Michelin brothers in 1895.

Today's advanced tires are complicated assembly products, with tightly integrated tread, sidewalls, bead, carcass, steel belt, inner liner, and other components. Combined with the suspensions, which are connected to the wheels, high-performance tires and wheels have made it possible for automobiles to move on paved roads at high speeds (e.g., 50–200 km/h). In other words, we can say that automobiles have very flexible interfaces with the road network, namely tires and suspensions, in the sense that the detailed design of individual models, if not their basic design (e.g., vehicle width limits), can be carried out rather independently of the roads.

Hence, the wheels are the oldest part of the automobile. Yet, interestingly enough, despite the continuous technological evolution of powertrains, control systems, and main body structures, the basic functions and structures of the wheel system may remain unchanged for a long time.

3.3.2 Body and Chassis as Integrator

The second key component of the automobile is its main body, which unites all the other components into one integrated structure and protects the passengers from crashes and various environmental hazards outside the vehicle. The main body of an automobile consists of two parts: the lower part, or chassis, to which the wheels, suspensions, steering, and powertrain are physically connected, and the upper body, which insulates those inside the vehicle from the external environment.

In the early days of the industry (late nineteenth century), the structural designs of the automobile's main body were based on those of horse carriages, which had a body-on-frame structure, or a combination of a strong steel ladder frame (chassis) and a wooden upper body. The borrowing of features from carriages was not limited to their overall architecture but also involved basic designs for the main components connected to the frame, such as leaf spring suspensions, steering mechanisms, and drum brake systems. The early automobiles were thus called *horseless carriages*.

For what concerns the upper body, the terminology adopted drew on expressions used in the manufacturing of horse carriages, such as wagon, coupe, cabriolet, and so on, even though the first automobile, the Benz Patent-Motorwagen, did not actually have an upper body. Customized upper bodies made of wood were fitted onto the frames of the early automobiles by coach builders usually working on carriages, and they introduced the aforementioned vocabulary too. The upper body of Ford's famous Model T was also made of wood, so its body shops looked like huge carpenter workshops.

This architecture of the early automobiles, the body-on-frame structure, was carried over to their successors, including the already mentioned Ford Model T in 1908, GM's all-steel closed body models in the 1920s, large American cruisers (such as Cadillac and Chevrolet) in the 1950s and 1960s, as well as today's commercial trucks, pickup trucks, and large SUVs. In fact, most of the profit made by GM, Ford, and Chrysler, the three historic US-based automakers, was generated from models with the truck-type structure. Indeed, these US automakers were architecturally truck manufacturers.

Later in the history of the automobile, another type of body-chassis architecture, monocoque or unit-body structure, was developed. Most of today's small passenger cars, including sedans, hatchbacks, and small crossover SUVs, have such monocoque-type bodies. In this case, like in the fuselage of an aircraft, the upper body and the under body (i.e., chassis) are tightly united into one integral structure. While structural rigidity and crashworthiness are ensured mostly by the frame, made of thick steel plates, in body-on-frame vehicles (e.g., trucks), they are provided by the entire body structure, made of thin (e.g., 0.8 mm) steel sheets, in the case of monocoque vehicles. Consequently, the main body of monocoque vehicles tends to be architecturally more integral than that of body-on-frame vehicles, other things being equal. This point is further discussed later.

In order to safely carry passengers at high speeds, automobiles must rely on strong materials and structures. Roughly speaking, a car's materials in weight are 70% steel, 10% plastic, and another 10% aluminum and other noniron metals. The first Daimler gasoline engine vehicle (1886) weighed about 300 kg and the Model T (1908) reached about 500 kg, but today's highly functional small cars are well over 1 ton, which is due, for the most part, to safety, digitization, and electrification features. Because of its batteries, a high-performance electric vehicle (EV) can weigh more than 2.5 tons. A recent small monocoque-body automobile with a 2-liter gasoline engine is 1.2 tons in total weight, of which about 30% comes from its steel body shell, 20% from the powertrain (engine and transmission), and 20% from the wheels, tires, and suspensions. Although the steel used for the body is getting thinner (e.g., 0.8 mm thick) and stronger, the total weight keeps increasing as safety and energy constraints, as well as the electronic controls, tend to make cars progressively heavier.

Since fuel efficiency came to the fore as a crucial challenge after the oil crises of the 1970s, making the body lighter without sacrificing rigidity and strength, needed for safety, became a top priority for the world automobile industry. Efforts in that regard include adopting thinner sheet steel, complicated mono-coque-body shells, lighter materials, such as aluminum, plastic and carbon fiber, as well as advanced welding and fastening techniques.

3.3.3 Powertrain as Provider of Kinetic Energy

Let us now move on to the powertrain, or the combination of engine, transmission and drive shaft generating mechanical energy and delivering it to the wheels. While ancient vehicles with wheels were pulled by human beings, horses, cows, and other animals, automobiles are moved by machines that convert thermal or electric energy into kinetic energy, such as steam engines, internal combustion engines, and electric motors. The internal combustion engine was the design of choice in twentieth-century automobiles, but it is predicted that, by the mid-twenty-first century, electric motors will either complement or altogether replace internal combustion engines in most powertrains.

Mechanical power was initially provided by steam engines (Cugnot's vehicle built in France in 1779) and electric motors (first in the 1870s), before internal combustion engines (gasoline engine vehicles by Daimler and Benz, 1886; diesel engine by Diesel, 1892) were invented in Germany. By the beginning of the twentieth century, the internal combustion engine, like that of the Ford Model T (1908), had become the dominant design (Abernathy, 1978). Daimler's first practical gasoline engine had only 1.1 hp, 462 cc single cylinder and maximum speed of 18 km/h, partly because it was installed under the passenger seat and thus could not be made bigger for faster speeds. In these early-day automobiles, the power of the engine was transmitted by means of chains, a technology borrowed from bicycles.

Then, a new vehicle layout and drivetrain system was developed by P&L (Panhard et Levassor, France) in 1891: the engine (3,562 cc 4 cylinder, 12 hp) was now at the front and its power was transmitted to the rear wheels by a multi-ratio gear box, drive shaft, and differential gears. This marked a turning point in the evolution of automobiles. Indeed, the vehicle layout and powertrain technologies of P&L were remarkably close to today's rear-wheel-drive cars. With much fewer space constraints in this new layout, the engine could be made bigger and stronger. Daimler's 1901 Simplex Model had a 6,785 cc 4-cylinder engine with 40 hp and 75 km/h maximum speed. The Ford Model T (1908) had a 2,896 cc 4-cylinder engine with 20 hp and about 70 km/h maximum speed.

The drivetrains of automobiles also evolved over time, from early bicycle-type chains and belts to drive shafts with differential gears, multi-ratio manual transmission with gear box (P&L, 1895), smoother synchromesh transmission (Cadillac, 1929) and automatic transmission (GM, 1939). Front-wheel-drive (FWD) systems with constant velocity joints also became prevalent in the small car segment around the end of the twentieth century.

To sum up, the internal combustion engine has been the dominant design of the automobile powertrain throughout the twentieth century and in the first part of the twenty-first century. Originally, the functional goal of powertrains was simply to deliver more power to the wheels but, as issues like oil crises, pollution and global warming have gained increasing prominence, the simultaneous achievement of high energy efficiency and low emissions of CO_2, NOX, HC, and so on has become crucial. Although auto manufacturers have improved the engine itself by developing advanced internal combustion technologies, such as lean-burning and catalysts, these conventional approaches may no longer be enough.

Hence, by the middle of the twenty-first century, automobiles with electric motors and batteries, that is, either EVs (with no engine) or hybrid vehicles (with engine), are likely to represent a significant share of global production. The revival of a once-defeated technology (EV) after over a century's interval would be a very rare event indeed in the world's history of industries.

It should be noted here that shifts in the engine mix are driven not only by technological advancements and the firms' strategies but also by various regulations introduced by governments (e.g., Clean Air Act in the USA/California and Air Pollution Control Act in Japan) or international institutions (e.g., Paris Agreement and UN's Sustainable Development Goals of 2015). These regulations are sometimes the result of complex political processes.

3.3.4 Steering, Accelerator, Brakes, and so on as Manipulators

The last set of key elements in an automobile comprises the means by which human operators control the wheels and powertrain. We may call these *manipulators*, considering that, since their invention, automobiles have ultimately been controlled by humans. More specifically, an ordinary automobile as a whole, if not its components, was not fully electronically controlled until, at least, the early decades of the twenty-first century.

Such manipulators include the steering mechanism, braking system, accelerator pedal, gear shift lever, clutch pedal, and ignition switch. Although the instrument panel features many other switches, meters, and monitors related to controlling the vehicle, here we focus only on those which directly help the driver control the wheels, engine and drivetrain.

Since the late twentieth century, these manipulators have adopted mechanical or electronic control technologies to assist human control, such as power steering, power brakes, automatic cruise control, and automatic transmission. However, as of the 2010s, human drivers, as ultimate controllers of the whole vehicle, have not yet been replaced by fully automatic driving. The diffusion of autonomous driving will continue well beyond the 2020s, involving complex interactions based not only on technological, economic, and managerial choices but also on social, political, legal, and ethical processes.

3.3.5 On-Vehicle Software for Controlling the Subsystems

The subsystems and functional parts of today's high-performance automobiles are mostly controlled by dozens of lunch-box-like ECUs, with microcontroller chips, huge amounts of software embedded in them, sensors, motors, actuators, in-vehicle networks (e.g., CAN, LIN), switches, connectors, and so on. Such electronic control systems developed historically from electronic fuel injection (EFI) in the 1970s, but now most functional parts, modules and subsystems are electronically controlled by a network of ECUs. Except fully autonomous vehicles (e.g., level 5) of the future, however, the total vehicle will still be controlled at least partially by human drivers in terms of starting, accelerating, turning, decelerating and stopping.

3.3.6 Roads as Physical Network

Let us now look at other factors that may affect the mobility function. Automobiles are heavy and fast-moving objects that require a network of reasonably flat, wide and robust tracks, or the road system, as their complementary good. The construction of road systems has typically been a public project worldwide. In the USA, it was started in the early twentieth century. Although the country already had national roads for horse carriages and paved streets in cities, the speed of cars called for a network of highways. The construction of ordinary national highways in the 1910s and 1920s and of interstate highways in the 1950s and 1960s was one of the largest national projects in the USA of those days.

3.3.7 Energy Supply Network

Another essential network for automobiles revolves around the supply chain of fuel, including gas stations. Gasoline was initially sold in cans in retail stores but, by the end of the 1920s, this system had been replaced across the USA by about 300,000 gas stations, with large tanks above or below ground.

Both roads and fuel supply networks are complementary goods for automobiles, in that they mutually enhance economic value, thereby stimulating demand. In the USA, while most of the roads were publicly constructed, fuel was supplied by large private-sector firms. Other complementary goods for the automobile include loans, insurance, repair shops, spare parts, accessories, inspections, car journalism, driving schools, licenses, and so on.

As regards electric and hydrogen (e.g., fuel cell) vehicles, we need national networks of fast charging stations. Such energy supply networks were vital for the diffusion of internal combustion engine vehicles, and this will also be the case for green vehicles in the future.

3.3.8 Traffic Information Systems

The final component of automobile technology is the information system relating to road and traffic conditions. This information system, existing both inside and outside the vehicle, relies not only on conventional elements (such as traffic lights, signs, 2D static road maps and traffic information broadcasting) but also on those using advanced digital technologies. The latter include real-time vehicle-to-vehicle, vehicle-to-roadside, and vehicle-to-pedestrian information exchanges through intelligent transport systems (ITS), as well as 3D dynamic maps, continuous vehicle-to-Internet mobile communication (infotainment), and so on. Information provided via these networks may be monitored and used by human drivers/passengers or directly by the ECUs of the vehicles.

3.3.9 Drivers as Ultimate Controllers of Total Vehicle

As already mentioned, despite rapid advancements in ECUs and automotive software, the ultimate controllers responsible for operating today's automobiles are skilled human drivers. After completing the official training required to obtain a license, drivers are expected to be able to control their vehicles through proper starting, accelerating, gear shifting, steering and braking manipulations, as well as by having knowledge of traffic rules, vehicle maintenance, refueling, and other activities. If automatic driving becomes a reality in the future, we will need to address the matter of who takes responsibility for accidents caused by malfunctions of completely automatic vehicles. At present, there does not seem to be a clear answer to this subtle legal question.

3.4 Functions and Dysfunctions of the Automobile

3.4.1 Mobility Service as Main Function of the Automobile

We now look at the functional aspects of the automobile. The main function, or service, of a family-owned passenger car is personalized mobility from point A to point B that is reasonably safe, fast, flexible and often enjoyable. As illustrated in Figure 11, this function of the automobile is generated by interactions among the vehicle's hardware as structural objects, its software for electronic control, human drivers as controllers, roads as physical networks, as well as energy supply and traffic information networks.

When the individual benefiting from the mobility function is also the driver of the vehicle, the trip is a self-provided service, which is classified as consumption in economics. When the individual hires a chauffeur, takes a taxi, or uses vehicle-sharing services, in which the passenger and the driver are not the same, the trip is recognized as a value-adding activity in the commercial mobility service industry.

Before the introduction of cars, personalized mobility was by and large limited to walking. In the nineteenth century, the diffusion of bicycles in some Western nations made it possible for many people there to enjoy personal mobility at higher speeds and over longer distances. Later, it was the automobile that significantly enhanced the speed and distance of personal mobility.

3.4.2 Huge Economic Value of Automobile Mobility

As of the early twenty-first century, there are considerable numbers of people worldwide, particularly in emerging countries, that want to buy, rent, or use automobiles for their personal mobility, although many also use mass transportation systems (e.g., over 80% of those commuting to and from the center of Tokyo use public transport). As a result, in the late 2010s, nearly 100 million new cars and trucks (worth nearly US$3 trillion) were sold annually worldwide. Most of these were private passenger cars, despite the fact that they are typically high-ticket items (over $20,000 on average). Also, the world's automobile-related service sectors, including transportation, mobility services, retail, finance, insurance, and so on, add up to over twice the size of the automobile manufacturing industry.

Simply put, the size of the world automobile market and mobility industry is an indication of the huge economic value of mobility services, either self-provided or commercial, as well as of the great attractiveness of the automobile to many people worldwide. Furthermore, the industry is likely to continue to grow (possibly 1–2% in annual unit sales worldwide) in the first part of this century, in spite of occasional shrinkages due to recessions, trade frictions, and so on. After all, human beings seem to be creatures addicted to long-range personal mobility for several different reasons.

3.4.3 Huge Social Costs of Motor Vehicles

On the other hand, the sheer numbers of automobiles in operation and their mobility imply huge costs not only for their users but also for society at large. In a sense, we may say that the automobile was born with a few *original sins*, in that it has a considerable negative impact in terms of traffic accidents, gas emissions, exhaustion of energy resources, and so on, and this will force the endless pursuit of automotive innovations during this century at least.

After all, cars are heavy, fast-moving objects operated by individuals in public spaces, and this state of affairs is not due to change in the foreseeable future. This combination of mass, speed, and space is often deadly, with over a million people dying each year in traffic accidents worldwide. In addition, as well as noise, pollution and other issues, nearly 20% of the world's CO_2 emissions come from the automobile sector.

It is true that, to some extent, new technologies and improved social systems may alleviate these problems. For example, Japan reduced its traffic casualties from about 16,000 to 4,000 between the 1970s and the 2010s and improved the fuel efficiency of gasoline engine vehicles by over 30% between 2000 and 2010. Nevertheless, from the society's point of view, no satisfactory solutions have been put forward so far. These problems of the automobile, together with many people's growing expectations regarding its mobility and charm, will require continuous innovations and lead to ever-increasing product complexity in years to come.

4 Product Architecture of the Automobile

4.1 Definition, Types, and Measurement of Product Architecture

4.1.1 Architectures of Products and Processes

We now analyze the architecture of the automobile. Whereas a product's *technology*, discussed in Section 3, is design knowledge about concrete causal relations between its structures and functions, its *architecture* deals with abstract connections between its functional and structural elements (Ulrich, 1995). As such, architecture can be defined for any given artificial system (Simon, 1969), including physical products, services, use systems, production processes, business models, organizations, and so on.

The designers of a new product start by identifying its overall functional requirement (e.g., mobility), derived from perceived customer needs and product concepts, and decompose it into a set of sub-functions or functional elements (e.g., speed) in a hierarchical way. They then conceive the structural hierarchy of the product (e.g., automobile), its subsystems (e.g., engine), and its components (e.g., pistons) as structural elements, establishing connections between its functional and structural hierarchies (Simon, 1969; Suh, 1990). The formal pattern of an artifact's structural-functional mapping is called *architecture* (Figure 12). Modular and integral architectures, discussed later, are two basic types of such function-structure definition of architecture.

The concept of architecture, expressed here hierarchically, is directly connected to our notion of *industry as design information flows among multiple hierarchies of productive resources* (see Figure 3 in Section 1).

A product's structure can also be described as a network of components, each of which has a functional core and interfaces, as indicated in the right portion of Figure 13. Where a product's functional and/or structural elements are interdependent, these components need *interfaces* with other components, through which signals and energy flow for mutual adjustment. A product's architecture can also

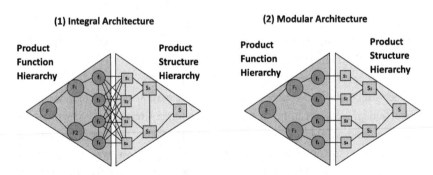

Legend: F = product function as a whole, S = product structure as a whole. F_1, F_2=subfunctions of the product , f_1 - f_4 = sub-sub-functions of the product. S_1, S_2 = large modules, s_1 - s_4 = small modules. ——— = connection
In order to simplify the diagram, the connection between F and S, and the same between F_1, F_2, S_1 and S_2, are omitted.

Figure 12 Product architecture as mapping between functional and structural hierarchies.

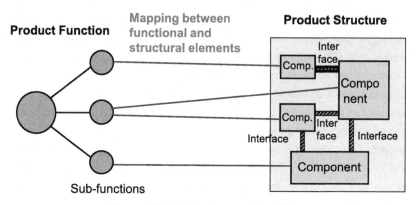

Figure 13 Architecture and interfaces.

be defined in terms of these interfaces. Open and closed architectures, discussed later, are two basic types of such interface-based definition of architecture.

The concept of architecture can be applied not only to products but also to production processes. *Process architecture* refers to the correspondence between the functional and structural elements of a production process. The concept of process architecture is important particularly in nonassembly-type industries, such as chemicals, steel, and other materials processing industries, whose products are monolithic and thus difficult to deconstruct into discrete components.

4.1.2 Modular/Integral and Open/Closed Architectures

As already indicated in Figure 12, there are two ideal types of architecture for what concerns coordination between an artifact's functional and structural elements: *modular architecture*, which tends to be coordination-saving, and *integral architecture*, which tends to be coordination-intensive (Ulrich, 1995; Fine, 1998; Baldwin & Clark, 2000; Fujimoto, 2007a).

Modular architecture, in its pure form, refers to a one-to-one correspondence between functional and structural elements. The parameters for components or production processes can be designed and operated relatively independently from one another, with less coordination among them. The *interfaces* among such components can be simplified and standardized, so *mix and match* of structural elements may generate varieties and changes of the total system (e.g., product) without sacrificing functionality. In other words, a modular product is *coordination-saving*.

Integral architecture, by contrast, represents a many-to-many correspondence between a product's functional and structural elements. The designs of the components tend to be specific to each variation of the product. Such components have to be optimized to the complete product through mutual adjustments of functional–structural design parameters. In other words, an integral product is *coordination-intensive*. *Mix and match* is difficult, and so is the use of many common components without sacrificing the functionality and integrity of the whole product. The same kind of classification also applies to process architecture (Fujimoto, 2007a).

We can describe purely modular and purely integral cases by using the axiomatic design framework (Suh, 1990). In this context, the design process is described as the design engineers' effort to identify and solve a simultaneous equation $Ax = y$, where y is the vector of functional requirements, x is that of structural design parameters, and A is a matrix representing causal relations between x and y, which are assumed to be linear for simplicity. Engineers identify functional requirements y^* given by customers and try to acquire causal knowledge A by learning from existing systems, accessing the scientific knowledge base, or conducting physical or virtual simulations. They then try to find the best-effort solution x^* by combining existing components or creating new types of parts. In this axiomatic design framework, a new product's architecture is summarized in the content of matrix A, which represents causal relations, where a_{ij} is a nonzero coefficient (Fujimoto, 2007a).

As for the interface-based definition of architecture, we have another pair of ideal types: *open architecture* and *closed architecture*. If the component interfaces are shared among different firms as industry standards (e.g., operating systems of personal computers), the product is of the *open architecture* type, whereas it falls into the *closed architecture* category when its interfaces are firm-specific (i.e., custom-designed for each automobile manufacturer).

Open architecture can also be regarded as a type of modular architecture in which *mix and match* of component designs is technically and commercially feasible not only within a firm but also across firms, thanks to industry-standard (i.e., open) interfaces existing among the product's components. *Closed architecture* is the case where the design of the product's components tends to be either firm-specific (*mix and match* is possible only within a given firm) or product-specific (custom-designed for each product model). The former may be called closed-modular architecture, whereas the latter is closed-integral. Thus, by combining the modular-integral axis and the open-closed axis, we can identify three basic types of product architectures (Figure 14): (1) *open-modular* (open), (2) *closed-modular*, and (3) *closed-integral* (integral).

Our design-information view of products, processes, sites and industries naturally leads us to adopt an approach to industrial classification based on architectures, in addition to a more traditional one relying on specific technologies. This architectural framework may provide additional insights into matters

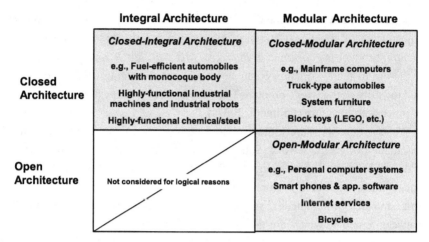

Figure 14 Basic types of product architectures.

concerning intra-industry trade and the theory of design-based comparative advantage, which we have already discussed in Sections 1 and 2.

4.2 Architectural Analysis of the Automobiles

4.2.1 From Technology to Architecture

As explained earlier, our design-based framework for analyzing a product has two aspects: technology (concrete knowledge of structure-function causality) and architecture (abstract knowledge of structure-function correspondences). Let us now go back to our causal map of automobile product technologies (Figure 11 in Section 3). By reinterpreting the technological causalities of a certain product into more abstract patterns of structure-function correspondences, we can draw a bipartite graph that shows its product architecture. Figure 15 presents two examples of such diagrams based on the author's best-effort estimates. It is worth underlining that the right-hand side of each graph displays product functions that are important to the customers rather than to the engineers (product cost was omitted for the sake of simplicity).

4.2.2 Simple Architectural Calculations

Figure 15(1) represents the case of body-on-frame (truck-type) vehicles that American manufacturers (e.g., Ford and GM) developed in the early twentieth century, when fuel efficiency and emissions control were not serious social issues. The diagram features 7 main components ($M = 7$), 3 critical functions ($N = 3$), and 11 links ($L = 11$) among them. A simple measure of this product's complexity is L, or the number of technological causalities to be considered, whereas a good

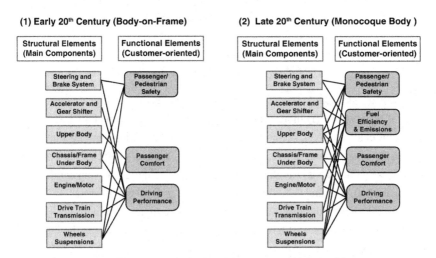

Figure 15 Preliminary analysis of the automobile's architectures.

indicator of its architectural integrality (inverse of modularity) is $L/(M \cdot N)$, or the density of its structure-function links; in this case, $11/(7 \times 3) \fallingdotseq 0.5$.

Figure 15(2), in contrast, refers to a typical small passenger car with lighter-weight monocoque body, more common in Europe and Japan. The automobile considered in this example thoroughly conforms to societal needs and government regulations regarding gas emissions and fuel efficiency. Compared with the previous example (i.e., the body-on-frame vehicle), its upper body is functionally much more important. Additionally, a new critical function, "fuel efficiency and emissions," has been added to the right-hand side of the diagram. As a result, the number of main components is still 7, but the number of functions is now 4, and the links between them add up to 19 ($L = 19$). The value of its integrality index is $L/(M \cdot N) = 19/(7 \times 4) \fallingdotseq 0.7$.

These simple calculations indicate that, as societal constraints imposed on motor vehicles (e.g., fuel consumption and emissions) have grown stricter in recent years, the design of automobiles has become more complex ($L = 11 \rightarrow 19$) and their architecture more integral ($L/(M \cdot N) = 0.5 \rightarrow 0.7$). It is interesting to note that even the architecture of early automobiles, that is, Figure 15(1), is much more integral than that of an extremely modular product with similar functionality ($L = 7$; $L/(M \cdot N) = 7/(7 \times 3) \fallingdotseq 0.3$).

To sum up, the simple architectural calculations just presented suggest that, even in the early days of the Ford Model T (the body-on-frame case), the automobile was more complex and architecturally more integral than many other products. And it has now become even more complex and integral, as constraints imposed by society on this product's *original sins* have grown stricter in the last few decades.

4.2.3 Conditions for Integral Products

Generally speaking, an artifact's design becomes more complex and architecturally integral when it has (i) more functional elements (e.g., specifications), (ii) more structural elements (e.g., components), (iii) more interrelations among functions, (iv) more interrelations among structures and (v) more interrelations between structures and functions. Among these conditions related to increasing complexity, we regard (iii), (iv), and (v) as shifts toward more integral architecture.

Thus, the socioeconomic environments that call for products with more integral architectures will have the following characteristics: (a) the customers-users expect more functions simultaneously from the product; (b) the product needs more structural elements (e.g., components) to achieve the required functions; (c) the customers are stricter about balances among such functions; (d) its structural constraints in terms of size and weight are more severe; (e) the level of customers' functional requirements is higher; and (f) the level of functional constraints imposed by society is higher. The causal relations between the characteristics of the selection environments, that is, (a)–(f), and the trends in product designs and architectures, that is, (i)–(v), are displayed in Figure 16.

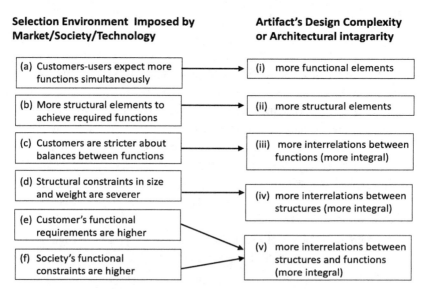

Figure 16 Selection environment that calls for complex integral designs.

4.3 Architecture of the Automobiles

4.3.1 Why Do Automobiles Remain Architecturally Integral?

From an architectural point of view, we can explain why the automobiles of the twenty-first century tend to be architecturally more integral than many other products. Some of the key reasons include:

(a) Customers-users expect multiple functions (e.g., mobility, self-expression, fun in driving, comfort, safety, environmental friendliness) from the same vehicle.

(b) A high-performance passenger car needs roughly 30,000 piece-parts, 2,000–3,000 functional components and several million lines of software code to achieve the aforementioned functions.

(c) As they are buying a high-ticket product, the customers tend to be fussy about subtle balances among the vehicle's multiple functions, or *product integrity* (Clark & Fujimoto, 1990).

(d) Today's passenger vehicles must reach a high level of fuel efficiency, safety, and comfort at the same time, which means that they have to be lighter, stronger, as well as roomier. Consequently, structural constraints, such as space interferences and weight conflicts among parts, tend to be difficult to handle.

(e) Experienced customers-users tend to expect this highly priced item to fully meet the aforementioned functional requirements (e.g., design, comfort, power, driving stability, safety, fuel efficiency, and affordability).

(f) The regulations concerning vehicle/passenger safety, gas emissions, and fuel efficiency are becoming stricter and stricter worldwide, because of the *original sins* of the automobile – a heavy and fast-moving physical artifact that is used by many people in public spaces.

Thus, the passenger car, whose features are determined by design selection environments (a)–(f), is a typical example of a relatively complex and integral product that has many functional/structural elements and interrelations among them.

4.3.2 Macro and Micro Architectures

Lastly, a product's architecture has it macro and micro aspects. The macro architecture of the automobile refers to its design's overall patterns of functional–structural correspondence and interfaces, whereas its micro architecture shows a specific component's internal and external architectural characteristics. While the automobile's macro architecture tends to be relatively integral, again due to strict market, environmental and physical constraints, its micro architecture may be strategically determined by the firms and designers themselves.

For example, while the upper body of each automobile model is highly integral and product-specific, its tires are externally (if not internally) more open-modular, in that their interfaces to the wheel system tend to be more standardized across manufacturers. The same seems to be true for the embedded software system managing the vehicle's electronic controls.

In short, although the passenger car's macro architecture is relatively integral, its various micro architectures tend to be somewhat diversified, with a range of more integral and more modular areas. The recent trend of digitization of the automobile (e.g., electronic controls, automatic driving, connected car, infotainment) may expand the latter areas, while its macro architecture is likely to remain more integral than that of most other digital products. Now that we have investigated the automobile as a product from the point of view of its design, let us move on to the analysis of the sites in which it is developed and produced.

5 The Automobile Industry as Value Flows

5.1 Design-Flow-Based View of Manufacturing and Industry

5.1.1 Industry as a Collection of Manufacturing Sites

Based on our bottom-up view of an industry as a collection of products and sites, Sections 3 and 4 analyzed the automobile as a collection of products, focusing particularly on its basic technologies and architectures. In this section, instead, we look at the manufacturing sites of the auto industry. In our design-flow view of manufacturing, the automobile *industry* can be seen as a bundle of flows of automotive design information to the market. Therefore, it can also be regarded as a collection of manufacturing sites, each of which controls a certain portion of these flows. For example, assuming that the annual world production is about 100 million units (as of the late 2010s) and the efficient scale of final assembly is 200,000 units per year (Maxcy & Silberston, 1959), it is estimated that there are at least 500 automobile assembly lines or sites worldwide, with roughly similar numbers in terms of flows of car/truck bodies. These manufacturing sites include not only vehicle assembly factories, as production sites, but also product development projects, suppliers' production/development sites, as well as sales and service facilities, as long as they handle certain flows of value-carrying design information.

Generally speaking, an *industry* is a collection of such value-adding sites, sharing similar product-process design information (e.g., the automobile).

A *firm*, on the other hand, is a collection of sites and headquarters that are controlled by a single capital. Whereas a traditional local firm stays within a country's borders, today's firms are, in many cases, multinational and multi-industrial (i.e., multidivisional). In the case of the auto industry, however, also due to its particularly large size (over $2 trillion), many manufacturers and assemblers, such as GM, Toyota, and VW, are heavily dependent on this single business, so we will simply call them *automobile firms*.

5.1.2 Manufacturing as Circulation of Design Information

Figure 17 summarizes our broad view of manufacturing as flows of design information that is embedded in certain direct materials as its media (Fujimoto 1999, 2007a; Fujimoto & Heller, 2018; Fujimoto & Ikuine, 2018).

The vertical flow (upper part of Figure 17) concerns *product development*, or creating the new product's design information, from product concept generation to functional design, structural design, and process design. At the end of this vertical flow, the productive resources – such as equipment, tools, dies, and human skills, which hold certain portions of the product's structural design information – are deployed to the shop floor. The automobile manufacturers also need to *purchase* direct materials and parts from their suppliers (left part of

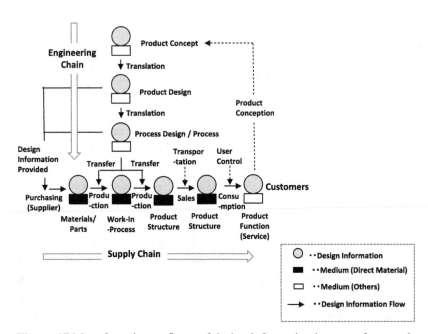

Figure 17 Manufacturing as flows of design information between firms and customers.

Figure 17). When the design of the product's parts is product-specific (i.e., customized), this design information is partially provided to the suppliers. As such, purchasing activities involve flows of design information as well.

Then comes *production*, in which the vertical flow of the engineering chain (product development) merges into the horizontal flow of the supply chain (lower part of Figure 17) and the structural design information deployed in the equipment, dies, SOPs, and so on on the shop floor is repeatedly transferred to the incoming direct materials as its media. The next step is *sales*. After production is concluded, the complete design information of the finished products is delivered to the customers directly or via sales facilities. Its delivery is nothing but the full flow of the automobile's structural design information to the customers.

Finally, as explained in Section 2, the customers operate the products' structures (in our case, by driving the automobiles), thereby generating product functions that are expected to satisfy the operators-consumers. This process of self-providing services is also called *consumption* of the product. Available information about consumption and customer satisfaction may be taken into account at the beginning of the next product development process, so that a new cycle of design information circulation starts there. If the automobile's function alone (e.g., moving fast and safely from point A to point B) is delivered by the firms to the customers, we call this business *mobility service* in a broad sense. Let us now apply this design-flow-based framework to the case of the automobile.

5.2 Product Development as Creation of Design Information

5.2.1 Large Project Size

Product development, which is upstream of the design information flow, is a project dealing with major model changes or all-new products, in which over 50% of the functional parts are usually redesigned. Since today's highly functional automobiles are architecturally very complex and rather integral, with about 30,000 piece-parts, 2,000–3,000 functional components and sometimes a hundred million or more lines of embedded software code for electronic controls (as of the end of the 2010s), an automobile development project is among the largest, as far as mass-produced consumer goods are concerned. Clark and Fujimoto (1991) measured the engineering person-hours required for around 30 US, European and Japanese projects of the late 1980s and found that the average project with standard content needed more than two million person-hours. When the author repeated this measurement in the 1990s and 2000s, the figure had gone up, apparently reflecting the increasing complexity of this product (see Figure 9 in Section 2).

5.2.2 Product Concept Creation

An automobile development project, as the flow of design information creation, consists of four stages: (i) product concept creation; (ii) product planning; (iii) product engineering; (iv) process engineering (Clark & Fujimoto, 1990). It starts from (i) *concept creation*, which takes place about three years before the product is introduced to the market in the case of recent Japanese models. Effective product conception is critical to the successful development of this complex consumer good, in which *product integrity* plays a key role. It clarifies how the product can attract and satisfy target customers in the future and brings about *product integrity* (Clark & Fujimoto, 1990), thereby raising the likelihood that the new model will be successful in the market.

Organizationally, distinctive product concept creation, led by the so-called Heavyweight Product Manager (HWPM), tends to enhance the product's total quality and integrity (Fujimoto, 1989; Clark & Fujimoto, 1991). The origins of what is known as *design thinking*, prevalent in Silicon Valley in recent years, can be traced back to what may be called *use-scene-focused concept creation* at certain automobile manufacturers led by HWPMs (e.g., Honda Super Cub 1958; Toyota Corolla 1966). A new product's concept may be expressed in various ways, including key words (e.g., "oneness between horse and rider"), critical numbers (e.g., fuel efficiency increased by 100%), imaginative sketches, or even short novels describing how future customers will enjoy life, thanks to the product. Concept creation by using digital/virtual models is discussed later.

5.2.3 Product Planning and Basic Product Design

The second stage of an automobile development project is often called (ii) *product planning* and includes specifications for key performance targets, exterior and interior design, vehicle layout, and choices of component technologies. At the end of this stage comes the top management's approval of the project, one of the most important milestones in the entire process. Although detailed structural designs (e.g., component engineering drawings) and fully-fledged physical engineering prototype vehicles may not be ready at this point, physical advanced engineering prototyping, 3D-CAD modeling, and virtual simulations through CAE may be conducted at this stage, which often makes front-loading problem-solving possible (Thomke & Fujimoto, 2000).

The introduction of the 3D-CAD system in the 1990s facilitated the early involvement of production teams in developmental problem-solving, thereby enhancing the manufacturability of a new product design even before completion of its physical prototypes. At a Japanese automobile manufacturer, it used to be possible to solve only about 20% of a new product's engineering problems prior to the creation of the first physical prototypes, whereas 3D CAD has enabled the resolution of about 80% of such problems, reducing the number of time-consuming prototype iterations and shortening engineering lead times.

Also, compatibility among the new product's main structural and functional design parameters should be checked at this point. Designing a new product is like solving simultaneous equations about its functions and structures (Simon, 1969; Suh, 1990), and it is vital to make sure that the equations can actually be solved before completing the product's detailed designs. This compatibility-checking system, which uses digital data, is sometimes called computer-aided integration (CAI).

5.2.4 Product Engineering

The third stage of an automobile development project is (iii) *product engineering*. After the product plan, along with the exterior styling of the vehicle, is given the green light, the project moves from the planning to the engineering stage. Following the basic information approved by management, the first activity at the engineering stage is developing *detailed structural designs* of all the functional components, followed by building *physical engineering prototype vehicles* that reflect such designs. These prototype vehicles and parts are manu-factured and assembled by skilled workers in the prototype shops, which costs hundreds of thousands of dollars per vehicle. Although CAE simulations are common nowadays, physical prototyping of both components and whole vehicles is still indispensable to test and validate the structural integrity, durability, functional performance, as well as the emotional qualities and potential market attractiveness, of this complex physical artifact. Even in the age of CAE, dozens of physical engineering prototype vehicles are built and tested, usually in two or more batches in order to deal with necessary design changes. Going through these *design–build–test cycles* at a fast pace by means of flow-oriented manufacturing is critical to shortening total development lead times (Clark & Fujimoto, 1991).

Another important element at this stage is the *early involvement* of *suppliers* in component design and engineering. The US automobile suppliers have tradition-ally tended to concentrate only on parts production, based on detailed structural designs (e.g., engineering drawings) provided by the automakers (provided drawings system). Conversely, for a number of historical reasons, the Japanese suppliers have often been engaged not only in production but also in the detailed designing of the parts, following the basic design information (e.g., functional specifications) prepared by the automakers. The parts drawings completed by the suppliers then need to be approved by the automakers for commercial production (approved drawings system; Asanuma, 1989; Clark & Fujimoto, 1991; Fujimoto, 1999). The two systems are compared in greater detail later in this section.

5.2.5 Process Engineering

The final stage of product development is (iv) process engineering. Such productive resources as production line layout, equipment, tools, dies, SOPs, and skills, which altogether carry the design information of the complete vehicle, are designed, built and deployed to the shop floor, so that commercial production can start competitively.

In the case of press dies, body design information in the 3D-CAD system is digitally translated into die design and toolpath information for die cutting, which is then transferred to cast iron to produce physical stamping dies. This process may be carried out in-house or by die makers. After test-stamping using try-out machines, preproduction using commercial press machines is started.

When the productive resources for commercial production are ready, the manufacturer moves on to preproduction of pilot vehicles, or prototypes, built by means of volume production tools either at pilot plants or at actual mass-production lines. Many pilot vehicles are tested structurally and functionally to determine whether the production processes for the new product have sufficient competitive potential in quality, productivity, and so on. Just like in product engineering, fast and accurate implementation of design–build–test cycles in the process engineering phase is essential for effective product development.

Another crucial point is *overlapping problem-solving* between product and process engineering, which may also be called *simultaneous* or *concurrent engineering*. In the case of body (product) engineering and die (process) engineering, die engineers start designing and making the dies at a very early stage, even before the body designs are finalized. This kind of effective "flying start" is possible only if regular communication and knowledge sharing occur between product and process engineers (Clark & Fujimoto, 1991).

When all of the necessary productive resources are deployed to the shop floor, the last stage of product development is ramp-up. To ensure fast and accurate starting up of high-volume production, the early involvement of production workers/leaders in the production process is of great importance.

5.2.6 Advanced Engineering

Another technological activity conducted prior to product development is *advanced engineering*, which develops new technologies that are integrated into the new products. As the product design of automobiles has grown in complexity over recent years, the lead times to develop technologically advanced components, such as hybrid systems and driver assistance systems, have also become longer. So, advanced engineering often needs to start before product concept creation. When this is the case, advanced engineers must be able to predict future trends in product development and achieve early coordination between the concepts of products and technologies, thereby effectively controlling the flow of design information between basic research and product development.

5.2.7 Emergence of Virtual Engineering

In more recent years, there have been two major trends in automotive product development, both of which are related to advancements in digital technologies: virtual engineering and embedded software platforms.

First, further computerization of product development processes (e.g., CAD, CAM, CAE, PLM, etc.), also known as *virtual engineering* or *model-based development* (MBD), will eventually enable reasonably accurate virtual testing (i.e., computer simulations using CAE) of total vehicle functions, with all five components (see Section 3) digitized through mathematical reproductions of the real world: (i) 3D-CAD structural models of total vehicles and components, as well as 3D CG (computer graphics) to visualize them as they will look in reality; (ii) 3D digital maps of roads and traffic infrastructures; (iii) in-vehicle embedded software programs for electronic control; (vi) digital models of drivers' behaviors; and (v) CAE models for simulating vehicles' functional performance and structural deformation (Uchida 2017).

Such advancements in virtual testing will make the functional verification (if not the final validation) of new products possible even before the actual testing of physical prototypes by human test drivers on vehicle test tracks. The virtual homologation of new products is likely to be approved by EU countries first.

Furthermore, virtual engineering may allow development project leaders to create use-scene-focused product concepts based on the digital data already referred to (CAD, CAM, CG, etc.) at the front end of the development process. That is, through the aforementioned digital models, (i)–(v), the product concept creators can "test drive" the virtual prototype vehicles in the very early stages of development, in order to see if they can realize their target uses in a real-life scene, while engineers, suppliers, workers, marketers, and so on can provide effective suggestions and counterproposals about these visualized digital concepts. This can be regarded as an ultimate form of front-loading problem-solving for design coordination (Thomke & Fujimoto, 2000).

5.2.8 Platforms for Vehicle Control Software

Another trend in recent years has been the creation of open platforms for automotive software development. As mentioned in Section 3.3, automobiles are, and will continue to be, equipped with large amounts of embedded software necessary for their electronic control. Its development now takes up well over half of total engineering hours, causing a rapid increase in development costs for each new model. Additionally, the autonomous driving cars of the future will require an even larger amount of software.

In order to alleviate the impact of its overwhelming complexity, the modularization of automotive software is crucial. Although vehicle control software as a whole is mostly product-specific, so that it can precisely control each model's hardware, it is often designed by combining open software modules that are developed by major electronic parts suppliers (e.g., Bosch) and used across the automobile industry. Such an open-modular system of complementary software blocks may be regarded as a *platform*.

There have been certain international and interfirm efforts to create architecturally more open-modular platforms, more like the ones used for PCs, with industry-standard basic software (including OS), standard interface, and more specific applications. AUTOSAR (AUTomotive Open System ARchitecture), a consortium-based standard for on-vehicle software developed mainly by European firms and authorities, is one of such initiatives.

Although, as already explained, the hardware of today's automobiles will remain architecturally relatively integral, automotive software may tend toward the open-modular end of the architectural spectrum. However, as of the early 2020s, whether these platforms of the future will eventually become global (open), regional, or firm-specific (closed) still remains to be seen.

5.3 Purchasing

5.3.1 Product Architecture Affects Supplier Systems

Let us move on to purchasing of direct materials and parts. In our framework, a product's development is the creation of its design information, production is the transfer of such design information to direct materials as media, and purchasing is the acquisition of such media.

The nature of a product's parts is affected by its architecture. For example, if a product's architecture is relatively open-modular (e.g., personal computers, bicycles), its parts are more likely to be industry-standard components developed by independent parts manufacturers (i.e., suppliers' proprietary parts). On the other hand, to the extent that a product is architecturally closed, its parts designs are more likely to be firm-specific. If the product is closed-integral, its parts tend to be not only firm-specific but also product-specific, with component design optimization. This tendency is clearly reflected in today's highly functional automobiles, which are complex and architecturally closed-integral products. Indeed, in their case, over 90% of a new product's parts are firm-specific and over 50% are product-specific, whereas fewer than 10% are standard or suppliers' proprietary parts (Clark & Fujimoto, 1991).

5.3.2 Three Types of Automobile Parts Transactions

Given that today's automobiles are closed-integral, with mainly product-specific parts, parts transactions between auto firms and suppliers fall into three main categories, presented in Table 1.

As mentioned earlier in this section on product engineering, researchers analyzing this industry have identified two main types of parts transactions for component designs that are customer-firm-specific or product-specific: ① *detail-controlled parts* are governed by *provided drawings transactions*, in which the automaker provides detailed design information (e.g., parts engineering drawings) to its suppliers for production; ② *black box parts* are governed by *approved drawings transactions*, in which the suppliers follow the automaker's specifications to carry out detailed component designing and prototyping, which the automaker subsequently approves (Asanuma, 1989; Clark & Fujimoto, 1991). Past studies have found that in the 1980s, Japanese automobile manufacturers, which used approved drawings in most cases, tended to outperform their US competitors, which heavily relied on detail-controlled parts.

As already noted in this section, *suppliers' proprietary parts*, governed by ordinary *market transactions* (type ③), represent only a small fraction of an automobile's physical parts, reflecting the fact that today's cars are not architecturally open-modular, unlike PCs and many other digital products. Table 1 offers an overview of these three different patterns of purchasing, which are internally consistent in terms of transactions, component designs, suppliers' activities, flows of design communication, types of competition, and so on. Let us examine them in greater detail.

① ***Detail-Controlled Parts with Price Competition***: Type ① in Table 1, or provided drawings system (detail-controlled parts), is a transaction type based on price competition and short-term contracts. Each component's detailed design information (e.g., engineering drawings) is created and owned by the auto firm, which usually invites many potential suppliers to straightforward price bidding. The result is often multiple sourcing of a specific component, meaning that suppliers can be easily changed because they do not have design ownership. Due to their apparent effectiveness in exerting price-down pressures, these internally consistent purchasing practices (provided drawings, price-focused bidding, short-term contracts and arm's-length relations) were widely adopted by US and other Western auto firms until the 1980s.

Table 1 Design information flows between auto firms and suppliers

Type of transaction	① Provided drawings transaction	② Approved drawings transaction	③ Market transaction
Component type*	Detail-controlled parts	Black box parts	Suppliers' proprietary parts
Product architecture	Closed (closed-modular or closed-integral)		Open (open-modular)
Component design	Firm-specific (common) or product-specific (custom)		Industry standard
Supplier's manufacturing job	Production	Detailed design + production	Basic and detailed design + production
Design communication	One-sided from auto firm to supplier	Mutual between auto firm and supplier	None: Product number, price, and quantity only
Ownership of detail design	Auto firm	Supplier	Supplier
Competition	Bidding (price competition)	Capability building (competition)	Market competition
Contract	Short-term subcontract	Long-term subcontract	Sales and purchase contract
Attitude	Arm's length	Mutual trust	Arm's length

Note: *Typology in Clark & Fujimoto, 1991.

② ***Black Box Parts with Capability-Building Competition***: When the Japanese automakers demonstrated their international competitive advantages in the 1980s, comparative empirical research identified certain internally consistent characteristics of purchasing activities and supplier systems used in Japan, summarized as Type ② in Table 1. This transaction type, that is, approved drawings system (black box parts), relies on longer-term contracts and capability-building competition among a relatively small number of suppliers with engineering capabilities. It was especially widespread among Western carmakers in the 1990s (Nishiguchi, 1994; Fujimoto, 1999).

In this case, basic design information for a new product model is provided by the automobile firm, whereas much of its components' detailed engineering design is up to the suppliers. Supplier selection is made on the basis not only of price but also of the components' design qualities and other multifaceted criteria, leading to capability-building competition among a relatively limited number of relatively competent suppliers (typically two or three). Thus, the ability to properly assess the suppliers' overall capabilities is key to an auto firm's competitive advantage.

The components' detailed design information is primarily owned by the supplier so that, once it wins a contract, it can achieve the status of single-source supplier, as long as the model remains in production. The supplier is therefore motivated to make large investments in physical and human resources to improve productivity and quality. In conclusion, type ② purchasing practices put less pressure on suppliers for what concerns short-term price competition but may give them stronger motivation with regard to long-term capability-building competition.

③ ***Supplier's Proprietary Parts with Market Transaction***: Type ③ in Table 1 is ordinary market transaction of standard parts developed by the suppliers themselves, but this purchasing approach is infrequent in today's auto industry since cars (their hardware at least) are not architecturally open-modular products.

5.3.3 Large Functional Modules by Mega Suppliers

After the 1990s, as automobile designs became more complex, car manufacturers increasingly relied on a smaller number of suppliers to deliver larger chunks of structurally united modules, including cockpit modules and front-end modules (bumper + radiator + cooling fan + lamp, etc.). Since these modules were bulky, the suppliers were often located on site (inside the assembly building), in site (inside the walls of the assembly factory), or near the site of the customer's assembly factory. Such structural modules helped the automakers save on assembly costs, but their impact on development efficiency was rather limited.

In more recent years, large physical modules that are both structurally coherent and functionally complete, including corner modules (wheel + tire + suspension + shock absorber + brake), have been developed not only by the auto firms but also by the so-called *mega suppliers* (e.g., Bosch, Continental, Magna). However, since an automobile is architecturally closed-modular, as opposed to open-modular, these physical modules are mostly customer-firm-specific.

In view of the physical complexity of automobiles, a winners-take-all scenario featuring a single platform leader is not likely to arise, while multiple platforms created by consortia of leading firms may emerge instead. In any case, however, mega suppliers able to develop and manage software platforms (e.g., Bosch, Continental, Denso, Johnson Control, Magna) will increase their power vis-à-vis the automobile manufacturers in the coming years.

5.4 Production as Transfer of Design Information

5.4.1 Transfer/Transformation/Transportation of Design Information

The next manufacturing step is the actual *production* of automobiles. In our design-flow-based view of manufacturing, production means *transfer* of product design information from machines and workers to direct materials or work in process (i.e., the product's media) on the factory's shop floor. More precisely, any production activity can be described as a combination of transfer, transformation and transportation of design information flowing among productive resources (Penrose, 1959; Fujimoto, 1999).

In this context, *transfer* means that the same design information moves from one resource to another. For example, a body panel's design information is transferred from a stamping die to a steel sheet at the press shop. *Transformation* means that the content of design information changes on the same productive resource or medium. In the press shop, the sheet steel receives design information from the die and is transformed into the body panel. Lastly, *transportation* means changing the position of design information together with the medium or corresponding productive resource. Moving the sheet steel from the storage to the press machine is, of course, an instance of transportation. Assembly operations are another example of transportation: two parts of the product (e.g., engine and chassis) are transported to an accurate relative position before being fixed using bolts. Bolting itself is precise transportation of bolts to the position of the holes.

Although today's automobile production involves highly complex combinations of mechanical, chemical, metallurgical, electronic, and other processes, it can also be described as a combination of transfer, transformation and transportation of the product's complex design information. Here follows a description of the core processes in automobile production as examples.

5.4.2 Producing Body Panels

The first step of production occurs in the press shop, where a series of stamping machines or dies transfer design information to the incoming sheet steel using over 1,000 tons of deforming energy. Heavy steel sheet coils are transported from steel manufacturers, leveled, cut properly and piled up for automatic stamping operations. A wide range of newer technologies – including AC servo presses for complex and fast stamping, hot stamping for deforming highly tensile steel and tailored blanks for stamping complex sheets – are adopted by advanced press shops. As stamping is a fast operation (e.g., over 10 shots per minute), it is often physically separated from the downstream welding-painting-assembly lines. By combining human skills and advanced technologies, today's competitive press shops can reduce die-changing times to a few minutes, effectively achieving small-lot production (e.g., 500 pieces per batch, or a day's requirement for an assembly line).

5.4.3 Producing White Bodies

The next process takes place in the body welding shop, where various body panels, including rear/center/front floor, engine compartment, side bodies, roof, fenders, doors, and hood are welded to a body shell known as a *white body*, which is a highly complex subassembly module itself. Today's monocoque bodies are made using 0.8 mm or even thinner sheet steel in order to reduce their weight. Spot welding (4,000 spots or more per body shell) is the most commonly adopted technology, but arc welding and advanced laser beam welding may also be used.

Welding is one of the most highly robotized processes in automobile manufacturing. Since the 1980s, hundreds of robots and automated welding jigs have been installed in advanced high-volume body welding lines, with automation ratios (in terms of number of spots) reaching nearly 100%. This contrasts sharply with the case of final assembly lines, whose automation ratios still remain below 10% (Shimokawa, Jurgens, & Fujimoto, 1997).

In the 1980s, many of the main body welding processes started to combine fixed automation (e.g., automated welding jigs for initial framing) and computerized flexible automation (e.g., robot welding for respotting). However, more recently there has been a move toward full robotization, which is flexible enough for totally mixed welding lines, with body lot size of 1, that can be synchronized to the mixed-model final assembly line. The problem with these high-automation lines is that their downtime ratios are fairly high (often 10% or higher) because today's automated machines are not very reliable. This is one of the main reasons why there may be 1 hour or more of white body buffer between the welding shop and the paint shop to prevent line stoppages in the latter.

5.4.4 Producing Painted Bodies

The body paint shop is a long line for the application of three or four layers of paint (e.g., electro-coat, primer, basecoat, clearcoat), for anticorrosion, surface smoothing, and aesthetic purposes. Since painting involves subtle chemical processes, its quality is difficult to control and the actual sequence of painted bodies may deviate from the planned one, given that sometimes as many as 10% of them may go through repainting. Hence, factories usually have paint body storage (PBS) of between 30 minutes and 2 hours, depending on their manufacturing capabilities in painting.

5.4.5 Producing Engines

The engine itself is a subassembly module, with many parts delivered by external suppliers, but most auto firms produce 5 C core engine parts (Cylinder block, Cylinder head, Crankshaft, Camshaft, and Connecting rod) in-house. The materials used are either iron or aluminum, which are cast or forged in advance. Then, these near-shape blocks are machine cut to exact shapes. Since 5 C are high-volume parts, they were traditionally produced on dedicated or product-specific machining lines with fixed automation (e.g., transfer machines) and annual production capacity of around half a million parts, but today's lines are more flexible and feature NC machine tools that can handle mixed-model machining.

5.4.6 Assembly of the Complete Vehicle

Final assembly of the complete vehicle is still a highly manual process, partly because the lightweight body moves irregularly along the line, much like pudding or tofu, which makes precise assembly operations very difficult even with advanced digital technologies. A typical assembly line with 1 minute takt time consists of 100–200 assembly stations, 5–6 meters each, but the lines have tended to become shorter in recent years, partly due to more subassembly lines, as well as to sequential delivery and kitting of parts, explained next.

Since mixed-model assembly is common these days, the question is how to provide assembly workers with different parts for different bodies. There are three ways: workers select parts from parts boxes on the spot (small-lot delivery for smaller common parts); the sequence of parts is arranged outside the assembly line (sequential delivery for larger parts); the sequence of parts kit boxes is prepared outside the line (parts kitting for smaller specific parts). The latter two methods can simplify assembly work and shorten the line, but higher productivity and accuracy of the main line may be offset by additional labor in the kitting and sequencing area. Thus, rather than assembly automation, the real topical issue for many automobile firms has been how to deliver parts to the assembly lines in a fast, efficient, and accurate manner.

5.5 Sales as Delivery of Design Information to Customers

5.5.1 Franchise Dealership

The most downstream area in the flow of design information (lower right part of Figure 17) comprises sales and after-sales service. Since these sales-service systems are directly connected to each individual local market, their characteristics tend to vary significantly across countries, although similarities do exist as well.

As a rule, automobiles are not sold directly by manufacturers but by a network of franchised dealers as retailing firms. There are cases of direct selling by the automakers (e.g., fleet sales to businesses, Korean market) or of distributors intermediating as wholesalers, but the manufacturer-dealer-customer chain has been the dominant mode of sales worldwide since the US automakers first established it in the 1920s. The dealership networks of such complex and architecturally closed products, requiring significant after-sales maintenance service, are, in most cases, auto-firm-specific, with franchise contracts through which the automakers control or influence the products to be sold by the franchisees, as well as wholesale prices, sales targets, trademark, advertisement, repair service manuals and other product-related information.

5.5.2 Multiple Functions of Dealers

While the main function of automobile dealers is selling new cars, which provides most of their sales revenue, they are also engaged in other functions, including used car sales, spare parts sales and maintenance service.

The structure and behavior of the dealers are significantly different across countries and firms. American and Chinese dealers emphasize sales from inventories (with delivery times between one and two months), whereas German luxury cars are mostly sold to order (with a few months' delivery lead times). Some franchise networks focus on customer satisfaction with the dealer, while others more simply concentrate on buying and selling vehicles without much consideration for the quality of the customer experience at their sales sites.

The Japanese-style system of franchised dealerships has been characterized as dense communication between the manufacturer and the dealers, as well as between the dealers and the customers. Their service quality has been recognized as higher, but their productivity (e.g., monthly new car sales per sales person) is lower compared with that of dealers in other advanced countries. Door-to-door sales have historically been common in Japan, while this has never been the case in other countries.

The Chinese automobile sales channels used to be fragmented, diversified and multilayered in the 1990s, but then multifunctional resale sites, called 4S shops, fulfilling the functions of Sales, Service, Spare parts, and customer Surveys, became the dominant model. The Japanese automakers (e.g., Honda) played a leading role in the diffusion of this 4S model. Since the 2010s, large-scale sites featuring multiple automobile selling firms, or auto malls, have also been growing rapidly throughout China.

The future of the franchised dealer system in the current phase of digitization is not clear. Nonetheless, we predict that dealerships will survive as multifunctional service providers, although their service mix may change. Carmakers' direct sales on the Internet may become more prevalent in the future, but local dealers will still be the product's physical delivery points. Their role in vehicle maintenance will continue to be important. The future expansion of car sharing and ride sharing businesses (advanced mobility service) may affect the dealers' sales of privately owned vehicles, but the mobility service firms' demand for maintenance of those shared vehicles may be very large, since their utilization ratios may be much higher than those of privately owned vehicles (roughly 5%). The user-related information collected by the dealers through direct customer contacts may still be valuable even in the digital era.

5.5.3 The Automobile Industry as Flows of Design Information

To sum up, we can see an industry as flows of value-carrying design information to and from the customers. It consists of various types of manufacturing sites (genba), each of which handles certain aspects of such flows. Thus, firms or countries that have more sites endowed with manufacturing capabilities are likely to gain competitive advantages vis-à-vis rival firms or countries. Now that we have briefly looked at the value flows of the automobile industry, let us turn to the main controller/improver of such flows, that is, the manufacturing capability of automobile firms and sites.

6 Evolution of Coordinative Manufacturing Capability

6.1 Organizational Capability of Manufacturing Sites

6.1.1 Manufacturing Capability Defined

Organizational capability is a concept developed in evolutionary economics and in the resource-based view of firms in strategic management (Penrose, 1959; Nelson & Winter, 1982; Grant, 2016; Fujimoto, 1999). According to this view, a firm or one of its manufacturing sites is seen as the holder of firm-specific (or site-specific) organizational capability, or a system of *organizational routines* that govern the flows of value added (i.e., design information) among the site's productive resources. The organizational capability of a best-practice firm is difficult for other firms to imitate, so interfirm differences in competitiveness stemming from it are usually sustainable over a long period of time. Also, organizational capability tends to be built up cumulatively by a firm rather than established through one major investment or innovation. The process of capability building is not always based on deliberate planning and may well be emergent (Mintzberg & Waters, 1985) or evolutionary (Fujimoto, 1999).

A firm's organizational capability may be found at the level of its headquarters (e.g., strategy formulation capability), but it also exists at its manufacturing sites (genba). When a firm's organizational capability for controlling and improving the flows of value-carrying design information to the customers is found at the level of genba, we may simply call it *manufacturing capability*. At all manufacturing sites, such as assembly plants, parts factories, product development centers, and sales-service facilities, the flows of value-carrying design information are controlled and improved through process technologies and organizational routines. The firm selects its core technologies, while its genba accumulate manufacturing capabilities, which in turn affect productive and other types of competitive performance.

6.1.2 History of Manufacturing Capability Building

In the history of the automobile industry, the production methods used to control value flows for total vehicle assembly have evolved over time in the following order: (1) *Static assembly*, in which a vehicle is assembled at a single workstation, while its parts are gathered from inventory storage; (2) *Single-model assembly line*, where the main bodies of a single design flow through a series of workstations with parts inventory storage; (3) *Multi-model assembly line*, where the main bodies of various designs flow through a series of workstations with multivariation parts delivery points.

(1) Static Assembly System: Stationary or static assembly was the dominant assembly method during the automobile's pre-mass-production era (1880s–1900s), but it continues to be used when many models with very different designs have to be assembled in small volumes. Thanks to its flexibility, this system adapts to a wide range of product varieties, but its productivity is relatively low due to its long and complex traffic lines, along which parts and workers have to move without adding value. In other words, the challenge is to manage the flows of incoming parts and the workers moving between the parts stock points and the vehicle assembly stations. Today, static assembly operations are still found in the so-called *Volvo System* for making special-purpose cars or in low-volume assembly shops for extreme luxury cars.

(2) Ford–GM Mass-Production System: The champion of single-model assembly is the famous *Ford System*, which was introduced by Henry Ford and his young engineers in the 1910s. Ford's Highland Park Factory featured moving conveyor assembly lines for the rolling chassis of each design (a variety of wood bodies were produced separately), mass-produced high-precision (i.e., interchangeable) parts of product-specific designs made using specialized machine tools, as well as high-speed press machines for metal forming (Hounshell, 1984).

The original Ford System was developed by trial and error through a series of production process experiments. Huge sales of the company's superbly designed product, the Model T (1908–27), were a key prerequisite for the success of this single-model mass-production system. It achieved extremely high productivity and short production lead time (less than four days from steelmaking to final assembly at the gigantic River Rouge Plant, with high levels of vertical integration), but it displayed low flexibility in model changeover (six months of shutdown for the transition from Model T to Model A in 1927), a situation which W. Abernathy referred to as the *productivity dilemma* (Abernathy, 1978).

By the mid-twentieth century, the Ford System had evolved into Flexible Mass Production, first championed by Alfred Sloan Jr. of General Motors (Hounshell, 1984). Compared with the original Ford System, the distinguishing characteristics of this new approach were: larger product variety (e.g., full-line policy), greater parts flexibility (commonly designed parts shared by multiple vehicle models), lower vertical integration, and faster model changeovers. Overall, this system was more flexible than the Ford System of the 1920s, but GM's production processes essentially featured large-lot or even single-model mass production for both parts production and vehicle assembly.

If N varieties of vehicles or parts are produced by M lines, where $N \leq M$, each line can be a single-model line. This means that, wherever the condition $N \leq M$ holds, an improved version of the Ford/GM-style mass-production system is feasible, or even desirable, in the twenty-first century. However, it is worth underlining that, in GM-style mass production, work-in-process inventories between the parts/module production lines and the vehicle assembly lines tend to become very large, greatly increasing total lead times (Womack, Jones, & Roos, 1990), which has been a major obstacle to the continuous improvement of this system.

(3) Toyota System: The best approach to flexible automobile production with multi-model fabrication and assembly lines is known to be *TPS*, which was developed in Japan in the late twentieth century and subsequently reinterpreted as *Lean Production* by international researchers (Ohno, 1978; Shingo, 1981; Monden, 1983; Womack, Jones, & Roos, 1990; Fujimoto, 1999; Liker, 2004). Compared with the conventional Ford/GM mass-production system, TPS is characterized by a larger variety of vehicles and parts, lower parts flexibility (i.e., parts commonality), higher process flexibility for product varieties (i.e., smaller-lot mixed-model lines with faster setup changes) and for production volume changes (e.g., U-shape machining lines with multiskilled workers), lower levels of work-in-process inventories (e.g., *kanban,* Just-in-Time, Just-in-Sequence) and of product inventories (sales-driven production), multitask operations (e.g., self-inspection, self-maintenance, multipart assembly workers), and higher outsourcing ratio in parts production and design.

International comparative studies carried out during the 1980s–90s revealed that this system – comprising many organizational routines (a few hundreds) that altogether support TPS, or flow-oriented manufacturing capability – tends to bring about higher levels of physical productivity, process flexibility, lead time agility, and manufacturing quality at the same time (e.g., Womack, Jones, & Roos, 1990). These findings triggered a boom in the adoption of lean production worldwide, also in sectors other than the automobile industry.

Two vital aspects remain to be explored, namely how Toyota-style manufacturing systems have evolved over time and whether their flexible manufacturing capability will continue to outperform other systems in the early twenty-first century. Let us now focus on the first question by introducing the concept of *evolutionary capability.*

6.2 Evolution of Coordinative Manufacturing Capability

6.2.1 Evolutionary Approach to Industries and Firms

An evolutionary approach to industries and firms assumes that the functions and origins of artifacts (e.g., products, manufacturing systems) may be explained separately (Fujimoto, 1999). In other words, an artifact with ex post functional rationality is not always designed deliberately by ex ante rationality but may be the result of certain unintended actions, such as pure chance and other kinds of emergent processes. When dealing with industrial phenomena of this kind, it would be appropriate to adopt an evolutionary approach to explain them.

We apply this approach to the case of coordinative (or collaborative) organizational capability, such as the Toyota-style manufacturing system (Fujimoto, 1999). Our assumption here is that this system is too complex to be explained solely by the functional intentions of its designer–creator (i.e., Taiichi Ohno). For this reason, the following paragraphs describe and analyze the Toyota-style system in terms of its structures (organizational routines), functions (effects on productive performance), and origins (the emergent processes that formed it).

6.2.2 Historical Background

Let us begin with a brief history of manufacturing capability in Japan's auto industry at large. Japan's automobile manufacturing initially developed from static small-volume prototype production and sales by small start-up entrepreneurs. When the Great Kanto Earthquake of 1923 destroyed Tokyo's mass transportation system, this was quickly substituted by buses based on the Ford Model T, imported from the USA. Both Ford and GM realized the potential of the Japanese market and set up their Yokohama and Osaka factories, respectively, as semi-mass-production knockdown assembly plants. They overwhelmed Japan's tiny ventures and occupied 90% of the Japanese market in the late 1920s.

The emerging militaristic government did not look favorably on the USA dominating the national auto market and passed extremely protectionist laws in 1936, which virtually ousted the Americans from Japan. The market and distribution channels set up by the US carmakers, mostly for trucks, were taken over by newly established Japanese firms, including Nissan and Toyota. Although heavily protected by the government, Toyota, among others, soon understood that the Japanese were far behind the US manufacturers in design quality, manufacturing quality, and productivity. Toyota's founder, Kiichiro Toyoda, assembled his workers immediately after the end of World War II, and said, "Our productivity is one-eighth or one-ninth that of Ford. Let's try to catch up in three years." Achieving this goal turned out to be unrealistic, but Toyota did catchup with Ford in physical labor productivities of main machining processes by the end of the 1950s.

Production expansion with product diversification was a distinguishing characteristic of Japan's postwar auto industry. Whereas the rapid expansion of the US automobile production from 50,000 to 2,000,000 units per year at the beginning of the twentieth century had been achieved almost entirely through a single product, the Ford Model T, Japan experienced production growth of similar magnitude in the 1950s–60s, thanks to the cumulative effect of a number of smaller-volume models. This historical imperative inevitably forced Toyota's manufacturing system to become flexible and efficient at the same time, deviating from traditional mass production.

In the last quarter of the twentieth century, the Japanese automobile manufacturers and their supplier systems took the lead in the international competition against North American and European companies in terms of deep-level productive performance, including manufacturing quality, assembly productivity, production lead time, as well as product development productivity and lead time (Womack, Jones, & Roos, 1990; Clark & Fujimoto, 1991). Among the Japanese assemblers, Toyota was one of the steadiest performers, with relatively stable profitability, large market share, performance improvements, and continuous capability building. By the end of the 1970s, Toyota-style manufacturing capability had garnered international attention. For instance, in 1980 Ford of Europe estimated that an anonymous Japanese producer's physical productivity (yearly production units per employee) was 3.6 times higher than its own, that is, 47 versus 13 (Ford-Werke AG, 1980).

The Western interpretation of the Toyota-style manufacturing system became known as *lean production* (Womack, Jones, & Roos, 1990). Firms that have tried to adopt this system include non-Toyota Japanese automakers in the 1980s, non-Japanese automakers in the 1990s, nonautomobile manufacturing firms worldwide in the 2000s, and nonmanufacturing firms, such as hospitals (i.e., lean hospital) and supermarkets, in more recent years (Womack & Jones, 1996; Liker & Ross, 2017).

As the lean system spread to the automobile industry across the globe, the gap in productive performance between the Japanese and Western firms started to narrow. The latter have improved their assembly productivity and manufacturing quality, but the Japanese plants have so far managed to retain their advantages. Consequently, Toyota-style (lean) manufacturing capability is still regarded as the best practice by most carmakers worldwide. It has also influenced some of the newer methods adopted by today's Silicon-Valley-type digital industries, such as design thinking and lean start-up.

6.2.3 Evolutionary Approach to Manufacturing Capabilities

Our next question is how this organizational capability was built up in the first place. Past research indicates that it was gradually formed in more or less emergent ways, which include not only deliberate planning but also unintended effects resulting from various forces and behaviors (Fujimoto, 1999). A complex organizational capability formed through emergent processes may be more difficult to imitate than a deliberately established one, because it is often impossible, even for those possessing the capability, to articulate it.

An evolutionary framework is a suitable approach for the analysis of such an emergent process, since it can explain the functions and generation of an artifact's structure separately (Fujimoto, 1999). In other words, to the extent that an artifact's structure cannot be described by means of a deliberate design process that starts from its functional requirements (Simon, 1969; Suh, 1990), we need to adopt an evolutionary framework that analyzes the structural, functional, and genetic aspects of the system before integrating them. Accordingly, the following paragraphs describe the structural, functional, and genetic features of Toyota-style manufacturing capability.

6.2.4 Routines as Structural Elements of Manufacturing Capability

Let us first look at the structure of this coordinative/collaborative capability. In the context of industrial/manufacturing analysis, organizational capability can be seen as a system of interconnected organizational routines, each of which governs flows of value-carrying design information among productive resources and eventually to the customers. For instance, according to Toyota's experts, TPS consists of over 200 manufacturing routines, each of which aims to control and improve such flows. These routines include Just-in-Time, *kanban* (pull system), *heijunka* (production-leveling), *jidoka* (automatic defect prevention), multiskilling, 5-S (sorting, sweeping, etc.), Total Quality Control (TQC), *kaizen* (continuous improvement), and other main subsystems, which can be further broken down into lower-level routines (Ohno, 1978; Schonberger, 1982; Monden, 1983).

It should be noted that most of these routines assume relatively high levels of teamwork among multiskilled employees, as well as dense communication and collaboration within and between the auto firm and its suppliers. We may call this structural aspect of the Toyota-style manufacturing system *coordinative manufacturing capability.*

6.2.5 Competitive Functions of Manufacturing Capability

The second component of our evolutionary analysis of manufacturing capability concerns its functional aspects. The primary function of manufacturing capability is to have an impact on the productive performance of manufacturing sites, or genba. As space is limited, here we focus only on the production side of manufacturing (see Fujimoto, 1989 and Clark & Fujimoto, 1991 for details on the product development side). From the design-information-flow point of view, the functional characteristics of Toyota-style manufacturing capability can be summarized as *dense and accurate information transmission among flexible (information-redundant) productive resources*. The density of information transmission from the production process to the materials enables both high productivity and short production lead time, while the accuracy of information transmission from the product design to the product itself leads to high product quality. All of this is achieved mostly through teamwork of multiskilled employees.

6.2.6 Productivity, Lead Time, and Transmission Density

The coordinative manufacturing capability at Toyota emphasizes increasing density of information transmission among productive resources, or reduction of non-value-adding time, when transmission of design information is *not* happening on either the sender side (e.g., workers, machines, tools) or the receiver side (e.g., direct materials, work in process). Non-value-adding time activities on the information-sending side (operation) include walking to go and pick up parts and tools, waiting for delayed jobs from upstream, setting up dies and jigs, dealing with defects and other actions. Non-value-adding time states on the information-receiving side (process) include inventory, queuing and transportation of work-in-process and direct materials.

Both physical productivity and lead time can be decomposed into speed and density of design information transmission, as the basic formulas previously mentioned suggest:

Physical Productivity = *Speed* × *Density* of Design-information-sending
1/Lead Time = *Speed* × *Density* of Design-information-receiving

In the case of modern production lines, speed is affected by production technologies (e.g., a machine tool's cutting and feeding speeds), whereas density is affected by organizational capabilities for streamlining design information flows, reducing non-value-adding time and continuously improving both design flows and productive resources. The Toyota-style manufacturing system is a primary example of manufacturing capability that emphasizes density rather than speed as a target for continuous improvement (Fujimoto, 1999). Thus, productivity and lead time are logically connected to flow-oriented manufacturing capabilities through design-information-transmission density. In other words, they are affected by both production technologies and manufacturing capabilities of firms.

6.2.7 Manufacturing Quality and Transmission Accuracy

Toyota-style coordinative manufacturing capability also emphasizes organizational routines for accurate design information transmission from the production process on the design-information-sending side (e.g., workers, equipment, jigs, dies, NC software) to the materials and work in process on the design-information-receiving side (see Figure 17 in Section 5). Also in this case, the combination of state-of-the-art production technologies (e.g., automated testing machines and artificial intelligence) and coordinative manufacturing capabilities contributes to higher manufacturing quality vis-à-vis rival companies.

The set of routines aims to ensure that the information-sending productive resources (e.g., workers and equipment) do not make transmission errors in the first place. This is the notion of *building in quality* or "getting the transfer right the first time," which contrasts with more conventional quality control relying on optimal inspection on the information-receiving side. When transmission errors do occur, Toyota-style manufacturers promptly react by collecting defect information through on-the-spot inspections, reducing inventory, and transferring work in process piece by piece to speed up quality problem-solving.

6.2.8 Increasing Density and Accuracy of Information Transmission

Overall, Toyota-style manufacturing capability in production can be described as a prominent example of coordinative manufacturing capability that attempts to improve *density* and *accuracy* of design information transmission among flexible productive resources. Also, as discussed earlier, coordinative capability is a source of competitive advantage particularly in those industries whose products and production processes are extremely complex and architecturally integral, including highly functional low-emission motor vehicles.

6.3 Multipath System Emergence and Evolutionary Capability

6.3.1 Multipath System Emergence

Now that we have described the structural and functional (competitive) aspects of Toyota-style coordinative manufacturing capability, let us move on to its generation, the third element in our evolutionary analysis. Toyota-style manufacturing capability gradually evolved throughout the second half of the twentieth century as the cumulative result of changes in individual routines. Yet, unlike the case of continuous process improvements (i.e., *kaizen*), it is difficult to find common patterns among these *histories of routines*. Instead, the overall process of capability building is seen as a complex network of events that include random chance, ex ante rational decisions, environmental constraints, unintended successful trials, unsuccessful trials, and so on. Such social system changes are mainly driven by intentional human actions, but they may have unintended consequences. The process of change may be explained after it happens, but it is difficult to predict its patterns beforehand.

Generally speaking, while the evolution of complex social systems or artifacts can be described as a process of variation, selection and retention, their variation, or generation, may be reduced neither to pure chance (e.g., neo-Darwinism in biology) nor to perfectly rational decisions (e.g., neoclassical economics). Let us call this dynamic situation *multipath system emergence*, in which variations in systems, artifacts, or capabilities can occur along multiple paths that include not only pure chance and deliberate decisions but also other intended and unintended effects of human actions, such as vision-driven or environmentally constrained choices.

In detail, the concept of multipath system emergence includes the following paths at least (see Figure 18): (1) *Rational calculation*, or ex ante rational

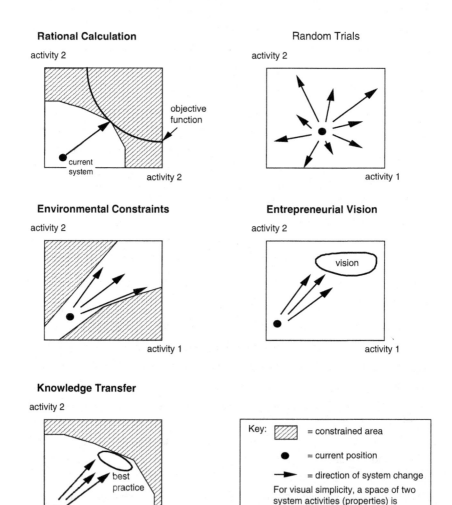

Figure 18 Multipath system emergence.

choices, in which the decision makers deliberately choose a new course of action that satisfies or maximizes an organization's objective function based on their understanding of environmental constraints and capability limits; (2) *Random trials*, in which the system may be changed by unexplainable chance events or random trials, as neo-Darwinism assumes; (3) *Environmental constraints*, in which the actors detect certain constraints imposed by the objective or perceived environment and voluntarily refrain from a certain set of actions. This reluctance may, however, bring about unintended positive effects benefiting the actors; (4) *Entrepreneurial vision*, in which a desirable set of actions is creatively chosen by the entrepreneurs based on their vision or intuition, without any extensive knowledge or analysis about environmental constraints (Spender, 2014); and (5) *Knowledge transfer*, in which a certain pattern of actions, or routines, is transferred from one organization to another, either through imitation by the organization lagging behind in terms of performance or through education by the leading organization (e.g., diffusion of the Toyota System to its suppliers; Helper & Sako, 1995).

To sum up, multipath system emergence describes a dynamic situation in which the observers cannot predict which of the aforementioned paths will emerge in the next system change. It is a complex and irregular combination of both intended and unintended system changes, as opposed to pure randomness (i.e., neo-Darwinism) or pure foresight (i.e., teleology).

6.3.2 The Case of Toyota-Style Manufacturing Capability

We now apply the concept of multipath system emergence to the evolution of Toyota's manufacturing system (Fujimoto, 1999). Table 2 reclassifies the types of paths of system change presented in Figure 18 as follows: (1) *rational calculation*; (2) *entrepreneurial vision*; (3) *knowledge transfer from other industries*, such as textile and aircraft; (4) *knowledge transfer from the Ford System*, as the preceding manufacturing capability to be emulated; (5) *environmental constraints* related to *rapid industrial growth under resource shortage*; (6) *environmental constraints* related to *forced flexibility* to cope with a small and fragmented market in the early days; and (7) *environmental constraints* related to *shortage of technologies* in the early days. The case of chance events or random trials is not considered, but attention is paid to whether Toyota has displayed the ex post *capability* to retain the organizational routines acquired through the paths of system emergence.

As for the organizational routines, our analysis takes into account some of the main structural subsystems of Toyota-style manufacturing discussed

Table 2 Main routines and paths of system change: the case of Toyota-style manufacturing capability

	Just-in-time	Multitasking with product-focused layout	Jidoka and flexible equipment	Kaizen and TQC	Black box parts	Heavyweight product manager
Rational calculation (Intended competitive effect)	Creating pressure for productivity improvements Throughput time Inventory cost	Productivity improvement	Pressures for quality improvement Flexibility	Quality improvement Productivity improvement	Cost reduction through manufacturability Development lead time and productivity	High product integrity Development lead time and productivity
Entrepreneurial vision	Kiichiro Toyoda, 1930s ("Just-in-Time" slogan) Taichi Ohno, 1940s–50s (system building)	Kiichiro Toyoda, 1945 (vision of rapid productivity catchup without economy of scale)	Kiichiro Toyoda, 1931 (vision of high productivity with small-volume production)			
Transfer from other industries	Textile (benchmarking of Nichibo) Prewar aircraft production	Textile: multi-machine operations in spinning (through Ohno)	Textile: Sakichi Toyoda's automatic loom	TQC was established in other industries (e.g., process industry)	Prewar locomotive or aircraft parts suppliers	Prewar aircraft industry (chief designer system) Forced transfer (collapse of aircraft industry)
Transfer from the Ford system	Synchronization idea from Ford (invisible conveyor lines) Kanban as incomplete synchronization	Productivity benchmarking of Ford Modified Taylorism	Adoption of Detroit-type automation when feasible U-shape layout as "incomplete transfer machine"	System suggested by Ford Training within industry Statistical quality control		

Imperative					
Imperative of forced growth under resource Shortage	Limitation of permanent workforce after the strike in 1950 Forced productivity increase in the 1960s	Shortage of investment resources: low-cost automation had to be pursued	Shortage of supervisors replacing craftsmen-foremen = need for TWI	High production growth and model proliferation created pressures to subcontract subassembly and design	Product proliferation with limited engineering resources created pressures toward compact projects
Imperative of forced flexibility with small and fragmented market		Forced flexibility of equipment due to small volumes		Product proliferation in the 1960s created pressures to subcontract design jobs out	
Imperative of shortage of technologies	Lack of computer technology for production control in the 1950s–1960s	Lack of adaptive control automation: *Jidoka* needs human intervention		Lack of electric parts technology at Toyota in 1949 (separation of Nippondenso)	

Table 2 (cont.)

	Just-in-time	Multitasking with product-focused layout	Jidoka and flexible equipment	Kaizen and TQC	Black box parts	Heavyweight product manager
Ex post capability of the firm		Flexible task assignment and flexible revision of work standards to better exploit productivity increase opportunities		Toyota maintained momentum for TQC by creating organizations to diffuse it to suppliers	Toycta institutionalized a version of the black box parts system that could better exploit competitive advantages	Only Toyota adopted the Heavyweight Product Manager system from the aircraft industry as early as the 1950s

earlier, specifically: (a) *Just-in-Time*, including *kanban* and small-lot production (Monden, 1983); (b) *Multitasking* of workers with product-focused (flow-oriented) factory layout; (c) *Jidoka*, including automatic trouble finding and line stopping with *flexible production equipment*; (d) *Kaizen* (continuous improvement; Imai, 1986) and company-wide quality control initiatives (*TQC*); (e) *Black Box Parts* transaction system with codevelopment of parts in collaboration with suppliers (Clark & Fujimoto, 1991; Fujimoto, 2001); and (f) *Heavyweight Product Manager* in product development, combining into one person the roles of influential concept champion and strong project coordinator (Fujimoto, 1989; Clark & Fujimoto, 1991).

6.3.3 The History of Manufacturing Routines

We conducted a detailed study of the *histories* of the main organizational routines of Toyota-style manufacturing capability, (a)–(f), and, in virtually all the cases, some or all of the paths of system change, (1)–(7), were identified. For reasons of space, the complete histories of the routines are not reported here (see Fujimoto, 1999 for details), but we offer some brief remarks on significant episodes.

As Table 2 indicates, deliberate capability building by *rational calculation* is consistently identified by the company in all of the routines' histories. After all, the auto industry has been an internationally competitive sector, particularly after the 1970s when the oil crises sparked international competition in the segment of small cars. Nonetheless, the rational pursuit of competitive functions has not been the only force guiding the generation and evolution of the routines. Other paths of system change, such as unintended *knowledge transfer* and benefits deriving from *environmental constraints*, are also observed in various forms, making the whole process of capability building rather emergent.

For example, the Just-in-Time concept followed the flow-oriented insights of Kiichiro Toyoda and Taichi Ohno, who also repeatedly benchmarked the Ford System and considered its application to the small and fragmented automobile market of postwar Japan. Benchmarking of prewar textile manufacturers, then Japan's main exporters, by Toyoda Boshoku (spinning and weaving) was critical for developing the idea of small-lot production. Furthermore, lack of computer resources and technologies forced Toyota to rely on paper-based production execution using *kanban*.

Multitasking across workstations was inspired by multi-machine operations in spinning. The bitter organizational memory of the 1950 strike, triggered by massive dismissals of workers, restricted hiring in Toyota's subsequent high-growth period, making multitasking and multiskilling natural solutions to forced productivity increases (i.e., "economy of scarcity"). Also, the flow management of the Ford System and the standardization of the Taylor system were always key targets in Toyota's benchmarking.

Jidoka and flexible equipment were influenced by the prewar invention of automatic looms by Sakichi Toyoda, in addition to his son Kiichiro's intuitions, while *forced flexibility* due to market constraints was another driving force behind developing these routines. Lack of advanced technologies, such as automatic restart of operation after the shutting down of a machine, led Toyota to opt for simpler machines with automatic stoppage.

Total Quality Control was established in other industries prior to its adoption by Toyota, whose quality performance had tended to lag behind expectations and be poorer than its rivals' in the early 1950s at least. Toyota was encouraged to introduce this practice especially after its leaders saw a similar system when they visited Ford plants in the USA in 1950.

Black box parts systems already existed in certain segments of the prewar locomotive and aircraft industries. Toyota's electronic parts business was separated from the company in 1949, in response to its financial crisis, and this forced it to rely on codevelopment of such parts with the then independent parts manufacturer now called Denso. Another reason behind the diffusion of the black box system was the shortage of internal engineers experienced by Toyota in the phase of motorization and model proliferation of the 1960s, when this resource constraint caused it to increasingly rely on its supplier's engineers. Yet, considering the levels of cost reduction and quality improvement achieved, thanks to codevelopment, this was, in a sense, an unintentionally beneficial course of action.

The Heavyweight Product Manager system, established at Toyota in the 1950s, had become an international best practice by the 1980s, but it first developed in the prewar Western aircraft industry, where it was common practice to appoint strong project leaders with concept responsibilities. After Japan lost World War II and the aircraft industry was banned for nearly 10 years, Japanese aircraft engineers, who had learned this management approach from their Western teachers, had no choice but to accept jobs in other sectors, including the automobile industry and the National Railway. Incidentally, those aircraft engineers who found jobs in the latter sector played leading roles in developing the Shinkansen (or bullet trains) in the 1960s. Thus, an inflow of jobless aircraft engineers brought about other unintended benefits to the Japanese auto industry, including the HWPM system, monocoque body, and aerodynamic technologies.

6.3.4 Evolutionary Capability at Toyota

In brief, as Table 2 indicates, (i) the main routines of Toyota-style manufacturing capability were historically generated by a combination of various paths of system change and (ii) no clear correlation was found between the nature of these routines (along the horizontal axis) and the types of system change paths (along the vertical axis).

We may thus argue that Toyota's coordinative manufacturing capability was built essentially through *multipath system emergence*, that is, the evolution of its routines cannot be ascribed exclusively to deliberate choices guided by rational calculation. In addition, as the bottom part of Table 2 suggests, Toyota appears to possess ex post dynamic capability-building capability, in that it often established routines, rules, standards, institutions, and so on ahead of rival firms, despite the fact that the latter operated in similar environmental conditions. When we observe that a firm has the distinctive ex post leaning capability of establishing a consistent set of organizational routines out of the situation of multipath system emergence, we may call this feature evolutionary learning capability, or simply *evolutionary capability* (Fujimoto, 1999).

Evolutionary capability is a kind of dynamic capability-building capability that works over the long period under the unpredictable condition of multipath system emergence. It is a nonroutinized capability, a preparedness of mind, as it were, displayed by an organization that tries to develop stronger manufacturing capability, whatever the situation, and includes the intended results of deliberate choices, as well as unintended successes or unintended failures. It is thus distinguished from routinized capability-building capability, such as that of continuous improvement (*kaizen*).

To sum up, we may argue that a firm like Toyota, which for a long time has enjoyed relatively high and stable performance compared with its rivals, tends to possess a combination of three different types of organizational capability: (1) *routinized manufacturing capability*, as the ordinary ability to repeatedly achieve good design information flows to its customers, (2) *routinized learning capability*, as the dynamic ability to repeatedly conduct continuous improvement activities, and (3) *evolutionary learning capability*, as the dynamic ability to create manufacturing routines in a more or less emergent way (Table 3). Toyota certainly possessed these three capabilities in the late twentieth century.

6.4 Conclusions

This section explored the evolution of capabilities in the automobile industry, focusing in particular on *Toyota-style coordinative manufacturing capability*. We adopted an evolutionary framework that explains the structure, function,

Table 3 Three levels of manufacturing capability

	Basic nature	Influence on	Interpretation
Routinized manufacturing capability	Static and routine	Level of competitive performance (in stable environments)	Firm-specific pattern of steady-state information system in terms of efficiency and accuracy of repetitive information transmission
Routinized learning capability	Dynamic and routine	Changes in or recovery of competitive performance	Firm-specific ability to handle repetitive problem-solving cycles or a routinized pattern of system changes
Evolutionary learning capability	Dynamic and nonroutine	Changes in patterns of routine capability	Firm-specific ability to handle system emergence or the nonroutine pattern of system changes in building routine capabilities

Source: Fujimoto 1999

and generation of the system or artifact in question. After discussing the history of pre-Ford stationary production, the Ford System and the Toyota System, we applied our evolutionary approach to the Toyota-style coordinative manufacturing system, analyzing its structure as a set of flow-oriented routines, its functions as the competitive effects of density and accuracy of design information flows, as well as its generation, which may be characterized by multipath system emergence.

The historical analysis of the main routines of Toyota-style manufacturing capability revealed that it was indeed developed through *multipath system emergence*, which implies that the generation of this system cannot be reduced to a set of functional or ex ante rational decisions. We also found that, in addition to *kaizen* and ordinary manufacturing capabilities, Toyota possesses a high level of *evolutionary leaning capability*, which may partially explain why its profit, market performance and productive performance have been mostly stable since the late twentieth century.

Within the context of this Element's capability-architecture approach to industrial competitiveness, the dynamic capability of a firm (Teece & Pisano, 1994; Teece, 2007) includes *capability-building capability* (e.g., Toyota's evolutionary capability in manufacturing) and *architecture-building capability* (e.g., Volkswagen's capability of vehicle design modularization), both of which are important for the evolution of an industry like that of the automobile (Fujimoto & Ikuine, 2018). The former is critical when a product's architecture is relatively stable, as the analysis in this section indicates, but the latter becomes more relevant when a product's architecture significantly changes. With this capability-architecture logic in mind, the following pages further investigate the past, present, and future evolution of the automobile's architecture and of the auto firms' architecture-building capability.

7 Automobile Industry Life Cycle and Architectural Evolution

7.1 The Industry Life Cycle

7.1.1 Brief History of Automotive Innovations

Having analyzed the capability side of the industrial evolution of the automobile, we now turn to its architectural evolution in relation to the industry's product-process life cycle (see Fujimoto, 2014, for a detailed discussion). We start our exploration with a brief overview of product-process technologies and innovations in the auto industry since the invention of the internal combustion engine. One of the key concepts is product/parts/process flexibility (see Figure 19), subsequently discussed in the various cases.

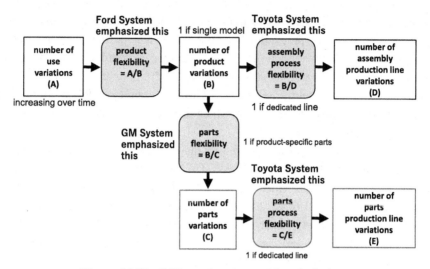

Figure 19 Flexibility and variety: a historical view.

7.1.2 Horseless Carriage with Crude-Open Architecture (1886–1908)

The two decades elapsed between the invention of gasoline engine cars by Daimler/Benz (1886) and the introduction of the Ford Model T (1908) may be seen as a period of rapid product innovations, both in architecture (e.g., P&L system) and in component-level technology (e.g., pneumatic tires), which transformed the *horseless carriage* into a fully-fledged automobile that was already similar to today's motor vehicles in terms of functions and structures.

In those early days, cars were mostly built by many small firms using a static assembly process. While there were many component-level innovations, the assemblers did not have enough production volume to order optimized custom-designed parts. Besides, the interfaces were not standardized and the physical shapes of the parts were not interchangeable (i.e., lack of machining precision). In such a situation, these firms had no choice but to buy components from the market, modify them if necessary, and then fit them to assemble the vehicle. We may call this system *crude-open architecture*, in that simple mix-and-match or plug-in assembly of industry-standard parts was not possible due to the lack of dimensional uniformity of key parts, unlike what we typically see in contemporary digital products and bicycles.

Today's cars are no longer architecturally *crude-open*, but an interesting exception is represented by automobile and motorcycle models developed and produced by many of China's local automakers in the 1990s and 2000s. Many of these manufacturers began to use copies of model-specific parts originally designed for the models of the automakers in advanced nations, reinterpreting them as generic parts, which they purchased from the market and assembled after certain modifications. We may call this approach *quasi-open architecture*. This version of the crude-open system was a natural consequence of the fact that China had previously had a Soviet Union-style national innovation system, with R&D concentrated at the national level and local firms focusing only on production. Acquisition of design information from abroad by either licensing or copying was therefore indispensable.

7.1.3 Ford System with Product Flexibility (1908–1927)

The following 20 years were the era of Ford Motor Company's Model T (1908), which dominated the US market, thanks to its superb product performance, as well as *single-model mass production* with precisely *interchangeable parts* made using special-purpose (often automated) equipment and high-speed moving assembly lines (e.g., one vehicle per minute). The Model T's extremely rapid sales growth called for the introduction of a mass-production system, which was established around 1913–14 at the gigantic Highland Park plant. The newer River Rouge plant was even bigger and more vertically integrated, with a dedicated steel mill in the factory yard.

Although the Model T, with its traditional body-on-frame structure, had various body types, from sedans to trucks, its chassis design remained essentially identical throughout its life. Thus, the Model T had a very high level of *product flexibility*, which means that a single product design could cope with many applications for various customer segments. The chassis itself was architecturally integral, with dedicated parts optimized for the Model T only. Its production lines were also highly dedicated to this single model. Thus, parts flexibility and process flexibility were very low.

Ford quickly ran through its learning curve and established cost leadership. In the late 1920s, however, new models produced by GM started to become more attractive due to nonprice factors, such as vehicle performance, additional functions and product diversity. After selling about 15 million units, Ford finally decided to replace the Model T with the new Model A, but this changeover required a six-month shutdown, mainly because the pervious production lines were specifically dedicated to the Model T (Hounshell, 1984). GM overtook Ford and became the world's top automaker around this time.

Ten years later, in 1937, another automaker with single-model (Type 1, or Beetle) mass production was established in Germany, that is, Volkswagen (VW). Over 21 million units of Type 1 were sold worldwide throughout its life (1937–2003). As for two-wheeled vehicles, Honda's Super Cub (1958–) has been called the Model T of motorcycles and has sold over 100 million units to date. These models and production lines may be regarded as the offspring of the Model T and of the Ford System.

7.1.4 GM System with Parts Flexibility (1928–1979)

The hegemony of the Ford System was replaced by that of the GM System, established by Alfred Sloan Jr., with its full model line-up policy, annual model changes (planned obsolescence), inter-model parts commonality, multidivisional organizational structure and franchise dealers network (Hounshell, 1984). The products' exterior designs transformed significantly (the fenders were merged into the main bodies during this period), but their chassis and powertrain technologies remained largely unchanged, except for automatic transmission.

The American automobiles of those days adopted a body-on-frame structure, as opposed to monocoque bodies. Such truck-type passenger cars were generally heavier, due to their size and thicker frame chassis, but low gasoline prices in North America made them marketable. Thus, a particular model's body design could be changed annually, while its chassis was not modified for some years. With common drivetrain, chassis, and other parts across different models and generations within a firm, US-made models tended to be architecturally closed-modular back then.

Because of GM models' high-volume sales and common parts, single-line mass production was still possible at the level of production lines in both vehicle assembly and parts manufacturing. Consequently, this system also adopted many elements of Ford-style conventional mass production. In other words, the GM System had higher *parts flexibility* compared with the Ford System, meaning that a common component could be used for multiple product models, but its process flexibility was still limited.

In conclusion, the pace of US automotive innovations in product-process technologies was not very fast during this period. Yet, Sloan's GM System was certainly a significant innovation in both business model and marketing. Essential elements of the GM System were subsequently diffused to other auto-making regions, such as Europe and Japan, and full-line policy and periodical model changes (every four to eight years) became common practice in the automobile firms of those countries. However, higher fuel prices made US-type body-on-frame passenger cars less competitive in Europe and Japan, where small passenger models with monocoque bodies – which were relatively light, fuel-efficient, complex and architecturally integral – had become market leaders by the 1970s (Clark & Fujimoto, 1991).

7.1.5 Toyota System with Process Flexibility (1979–)

When the second oil crisis hit the world auto market in 1979, the American automakers, which had coped with the first oil crisis by producing downsized versions of traditional large body-on-frame vehicles, recognized that their domestic product mix had to be shifted toward even smaller cars, with smaller engines and monocoque bodies. Therefore, they entered this market segment in North America, where Japanese automakers had already occupied large shares, and the so-called *small car war* broke out worldwide. However, having always specialized in large body-on-frame vehicles, the US manufacturers were not so competent at producing small-integral vehicles throughout this period. In the late 2010s, for instance, GM launched its global strategy apparently focusing only on modular products and technologies, including pickup trucks, large SUVs, range extender vehicles, and autonomous driving systems.

This was also the period when the so-called Toyota System, with relatively high *process flexibility*, demonstrated its competitiveness. The US government and automakers adopted all the available measures in terms of competition/conflict/cooperation, including domestic development of small cars (e.g., GM's X-body cars and J-body cars), virtual import volume restrictions of Japanese passenger cars (1982), and alliances with Japanese firms (e.g., GM-Toyota joint venture), but they could not stop their market share erosion. Nonetheless, the US automakers were still competitive in larger body-on-frame vehicles (e.g., pickup trucks for passengers, truck-type SUVs, minivans), where they retained their design-based comparative advantage.

Much of the competitive strength of the Japanese automobile manufacturers came from their manufacturing capabilities, with high *process flexibility*, physical productivity, conformance quality, and short lead times, called the Toyota System, Lean System, and so on (Monden, 1983; Womack, Jones, & Roos, 1990; Fujimoto, 1999). As discussed in Section 6, this coordinative manufacturing system was the result of the Japanese firms' capability-building capability, historical imperatives (e.g., small domestic market, rapid growth via many structurally unrelated product models, chronic labor shortage), and entrepreneurial vision.

Although the Japanese market was small in the 1950s and 1960s, the local automakers there still needed a diversified model mix to satisfy their customers. Opportunities to pursue parts commonality were scarce, as their products were rather integral in order to cope with ever stricter safety/environmental/energy constraints. Such limitations in product flexibility and parts flexibility forced Toyota and the other Japanese firms of those days to concentrate on *process flexibility*, which ironically became their source of strength. Also, due to the smaller production volumes of many models with lower parts commonality, *mixed-model mass production* was often necessary in final assembly and developed into different approaches. For instance, assuming that a Japanese carmaker needs to mix a larger model L and a smaller model S, the Toyota-style approach adopts levelization of production in sequences like LSLSLSLS and uses *kanban* (pull system) to purchase the required parts, whereas Honda applies a batching approach like LLLLSSSS and moves the workers around to absorb the gap in person-hours per vehicle between L and S.

During this period of increasingly intense competition and constraints, coordinative manufacturing capability for process flexibility, productivity, quality, and speed in developing and producing integral products has been a key element of competitive advantage. Also, for historical reasons related to planned and forced capability building, the Japanese automakers have tended to maintain their design-based comparative advantage. This, however, does not mean that Ford-style mass production and GM-style parts commonality are no longer important. On the contrary, when automakers produce highly competitive general-purpose models with product flexibility (e.g., pickup trucks by US companies, Korean compact sedans for emerging markets), they can still enjoy the benefits of straightforward mass production following the Ford System. Whenever a set of products has opportunities for components/modules/subsystems communization, either within a firm or throughout the industry, GM-style parts flexibility should be pursued. VW's common platform (1990s) and common module (2010s) strategies are among such examples. It is worth underlining that parts commonality is an old strategy, dating back to Singer's sewing machines of the nineteenth century (Hounshell, 1984).

To sum up, from the architecture-capability point of view, the world auto industry may be characterized as a combination of strategies to pursue product flexibility (Ford System), parts flexibility (GM System), and process flexibility (Toyota System), but these three stages are overlapped cumulatively rather than sequentially. Let us now move on to a theoretical interpretation of these evolutionary processes of the automobile industry.

7.1.6 Abernathy-Utterback Model

A widely known framework describing the dynamic patterns of industrial evolution is the Abernathy-Utterback model of *product-process life cycle*

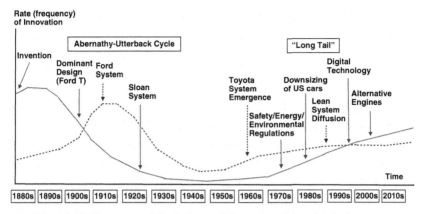

Figure 20 The automobile industry life cycle: a hypothetical pattern.

(Figure 20; Abernathy, 1978; Abernathy & Utterback, 1978; Clark, 1985). It hypothesizes that an industry begins with the invention of a seminal but functionally premature product model (e.g., the 1886 Daimler and Benz vehicles), followed by a wave of product innovations that improve the product's functionality, mostly using versatile workers and general-purpose machines/ materials that help absorb such rapid design evolution.

7.1.7 From Dominant Design to Maturity

During this *fluid* stage, the customers tend to be fewer, richer, and product function-oriented, rather than price-sensitive. As the products grow more conceptually articulated and functionally sophisticated, a highly competitive model that crystallizes past product innovations is eventually introduced to the mass market (e.g., the 1908 Ford Model T). Also called the *dominant design*, this standard-setting and concept-articulating model becomes a turning point for the industry as a whole.

The focus of competition then begins to move from functional performance to price-cost reduction, as the competing models grow less differentiated in their functional–structural designs. Uncertainty regarding product design decreases, so that heavier investments in product-specific process technologies and equipment become economically justified and a wave of process innovations soon follows (e.g., the so-called Ford System), while product innovations are less frequent. At this *specific* stage of the industry life cycle, products become more standardized, whereas production equipment, materials, components, and work skills are more product-specific. The focus of competition now shifts to economies of scale. Productivity goes up, but both product and process innovations lose their momentum – what Abernathy called the *productivity dilemma*. On the whole, the product-process life cycle model is graphically illustrated by two overlapping waves of innovation, in which the peak of the first wave, representing the frequency of product innovations, is followed by the peak of the second wave, referring to process innovations, with the dominant design placed between the two peaks (see left-hand side area of Figure 20).

As Abernathy (1978) explained in detail, the industry life cycle model fits the world automobile industry very well when it comes to the early phase between the 1880s (invention of an automobile with internal combustion engine) and the 1920s (end of Ford Model T production) – and even into the 1960s in the case of the US auto industry, in which product differentiation continued without significant product/process innovations (e.g., GM's policies of full model line-up and annual model changes). But this framework has not been equally successful in explaining the industry's product-process evolution after the 1970s, when in many countries society started to demand stricter constraints regarding traffic safety, energy consumption, and gas emissions. We propose the hypothesis of a *long tail* of the product-process life cycle, which means that these ever stricter constraints call for a high and long-lasting innovation plateau to overcome them. We also consider the impact of the long-tail product-process life cycle on the product architecture of the automobile.

7.2 The Long Tail of the Auto Industry Life Cycle

7.2.1 Rapid Evolution rather than Dematurity

Let us take a brief look at what happened to the global auto industry between the 1970s and the 2010s. These decades can be regarded as a period of *rapid incremental innovations* (Clark & Fujimoto, 1991). One may argue that a phase of revolutionary innovations may soon transform the industry, with EVs, autonomous driving and connected cars – yet, as of the end of the 2010s, this argument is nothing more than speculation about a possible future. So, for now we focus on the last 50 years, leaving the issue of the future of the automobile for my future publications.

On the one hand, product-process innovations have not changed the overall architecture or basic structure of the automobile, also including advanced EVs. Technological changes have been evolutionary rather than revolutionary in nature, meaning that they have not rendered previous products obsolete but have rather strengthened their functionalities and competitiveness. Consequently, the innovations of this period have not been wholly disruptive

(Christensen, 1997) and most of the main auto manufacturers have survived (unlike high-tech digital businesses over the same period), although some have been technically bankrupted and others have merged or allied themselves with their competitors. Overall, the average price of an automobile has not changed dramatically (roughly around $20,000 for a compact car after considering inflation) and there have been no drastic reductions in the number of parts and components per vehicle.

On the other hand, technological developments in the global auto industry have been sustained since at least the 1970s. The major auto manufacturers in the USA, Europe, and Japan have spent between 3 and 5% of their sales revenue on R&D throughout this period. The cars from 1960 and those from 2010 may look alike in terms of product architecture, exterior/interior shapes and basic functionalities, but the latter have improved dramatically in terms of engine performance, comfort, safety and fuel efficiency, as well as friendliness to passengers and the environment.

7.2.2 Constraint-Driven Innovations

Such rapid functional improvements have been achieved through significant technological changes in the structural components of vehicles and the way in which those components are interconnected (i.e., architecture), as well as through the massive introduction of ECUs with millions of lines of embedded software. This vast technological change is still ongoing. Hence, highly functional cars in advanced nations, with ever more demanding users and stricter environmental/safety regulations, are now overwhelmingly complex, which causes many design-quality problems for major manufacturers (MacDuffie & Fujimoto, 2010).

At the same time, since the beginning of this century, there has been an explosive growth in the emerging auto markets (including China), where the customers, most of whom are first-time car owners, generally prefer much simpler and cheaper models than those suited to advanced markets. However, this has not resulted in any massive attack of disruptive or revolutionary technologies by the newcomers. The segment of large automobiles in those countries is still dominated by the simplified models and technologies of existing multinational automakers, with Chinese, Indian, and other local manufacturers having gained rather small market shares so far.

Progress has been far from stagnant also in process innovations and manufacturing capability building. Various new production systems and technologies have been proposed since the introduction of the Ford System in the 1920s, which was extremely efficient and fast but not flexible (Abernathy,

1978). Influential examples include flexible machining, assembly automation (Shimokawa, Jurgens, & Fujimoto, 1997), the Volvo System, TQC, the Toyota/ Lean System (Monden, 1983; Cusumano, 1985; Womack, Jones, & Roos, 1990; Fujimoto, 1999; etc.), and integrative product development (Clark & Fujimoto, 1991; Cusumano & Nobeoka, 1998).

To sum up, I argue that the evolution of the world automobile industry over the past 50 years has been characterized by the *long tail of the industry life cycle*, with a somewhat upward trend of technological advancement (Figure 20), rather than by the simple end of one product-process life cycle (i.e., long-range technological stagnation) or the beginning of another, renewed cycle called *dematurity* (Abernathy, Clark, & Kantrow, 1983).

7.2.3 Neither Concentration nor Disruption

As for the global industrial structure of the sector, some claimed that the burden of huge R&D and capital investments would allow only about 10 major automobile companies to survive, but so far that prediction has never come true. What has actually been created over the last 50 years is an almost seamless network of international interfirm alliances and capital/technical tie-ups (Fujimoto, 2007b), involving dozens of carmakers worldwide, although the top 10 groups do occupy about 70% of the world market.

Others have supported the idea of *dematurity*, or disruptive technology hypothesis. For instance, in the early 1980s, when the US market faced a rapid increase in gas prices after the second oil crisis, R&D investments in various nontraditional vehicles (e.g., steam, gas-turbine, electric, nuclear, etc.) attracted popular attention, and some journalists even advocated a "reinvention" of the automobile. But that has never happened either. In the end, the most appropriate interpretation of the historical reality of the period between the 1970s and the 2010s seems to be found in the concept of the long tail of the industry life cycle, with rapid incremental innovations.

One remaining question concerns what will happen in the coming decades (2020s–30s), that is, whether the gradual expansion of constraint-driven innovations (long tail) will continue or whether another wave of the Abernathy-Utterback cycle (dematurity) will be triggered by the cumulative effects of innovations in Internet connectivity, autonomous driving, digitized mobility services, advanced EVs, and so on. I will discuss this issue in my future publications.

7.3 Integrating Industry Life Cycle and Architectural Evolution

7.3.1 Architectural Sequence in the Industry Life Cycle

Let us now combine the Abernathy-Utterback theory of product-process life cycle with the framework of capability-architecture evolution proposed in this Element. To this end, it is worth comparing the architectural evolution of the automobile and the computer (Figure 21). These diagrams suggest that the computer systems of future automobiles might be architecturally shifted toward the open architecture side.

As is well known, the industrial history of the automobile started with the horseless carriage, a rather *crudely open-modular* product that employed a combination of newly designed engines and existing/modified parts from horse carriages and bicycles (Abernathy, 1978; Hounshell, 1984). The dominant design, Ford's Model T, was highly integral, with product-specific parts, as far as its chassis, engine and drivetrain were concerned. On the contrary, its body-on-frame structure allowed for the development of various types of wooden bodies (e.g., sedan, open body, coupe, truck), many of which were manufactured by third parties outside Ford. Later, GM's common parts policy under Alfred Sloan, Jr. made the architecture of automobiles more *closed-modular*. A typical new model sold in the advanced markets today – with less than 10% generic parts, less than 50% firm-specific common parts, and over 50% model-specific parts – falls somewhere between the closed-integral (monocoque body) and closed-modular (body-on-frame) architecture (Figure 21). It should be noted here that most of the profitable models designed by US automakers, from the Model T to the pickup trucks of the 2010s, have truck-type body-on-frame structures (i.e., more modular),

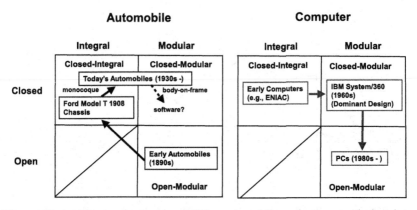

Figure 21 Architectural sequences of the automobile and computer industries.

whereas most of the successful high-volume models created in Europe, Japan, and Korea have monocoque bodies (i.e., more integral).

The architectural evolution of computers has been very different. First-generation machines (e.g., ENIAC) were highly integral, with model-specific circuits, while the dominant design, IBM's System/360, produced in the 1960s, can be regarded as a closed-modular model with an IBM-specific operating system (Freeman, 1982; Baldwin & Clark, 2000). But then came personal computers, which are architecturally open-modular with their industry-standard OS and CPU. Thus, the architectural sequence of the automobile, with functionally and structurally similar ancestors such as carriages and bicycles, has been open-modular ⇒ closed-integral ⇒ closed-modular/integral, whereas that of the computer, without such predecessors, has been closed-integral ⇒ closed-modular ⇒ open-modular.

7.3.2 Function-Price Frontiers and Customer Preferences

The architectural sequences and the *long tail* can be explained using the logic of capability-architecture evolution. It is best to begin with a Lancaster-type analysis (Lancaster, 1966) of the *function-price frontier* for a given product category with functionally equivalent models (e.g., compact passenger cars). According to this approach, customers with different preferences regarding a product's functionality and price will have indifference curves of different shapes: a *price-oriented customer* will have a relatively flat curve in the function-price space, while a *function-oriented customer* will be characterized by a steeper curve (Figure 22). As Lancaster does, it can also be assumed that

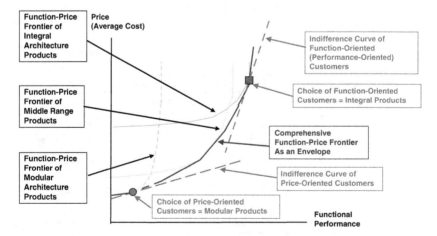

Figure 22 Cost-performance frontiers, customer preferences, and choices of architecture for a given product category.

a customer will choose the product that is located at the point of tangency between the product's function-price frontier and the customer's indifference curve.

Furthermore, design and architectural theories show that, within a given category, the function-price frontiers of integral models and modular models are different. The development of integral products incurs higher fixed coordination costs but offers better functionality due to optimization, whereas coordination-saving modular products enjoy lower fixed coordination costs but offer lower functional performance because of their mix-and-match nature. The set of frontiers of different shapes can be seen as an envelope that contains all the different architectures. Consequently, our framework predicts that price-oriented customers will tend to choose relatively modular products, whereas function-oriented customers will likely opt for relatively integral products, other things (e.g., production volume) being equal.

7.3.3 Explaining the Architectural Sequence

The hypothetical sequences of customers' architectural choices in the automobile and computer industries, shown in Figure 23, may help explain why the industry life cycles of different products display different architectural sequences. In this evolutionary setting, a product category's function-price frontiers, with product and process innovations, tend to shift toward the lower right portion of the diagram.

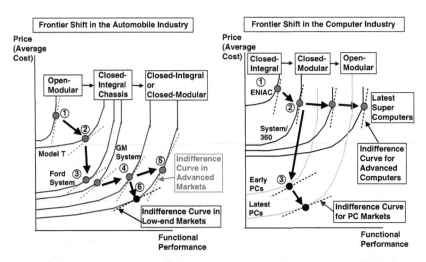

Figure 23 Shift of price-function frontiers and architectural sequences in industry life cycles.

In the case of the automobile industry, the initial frontier of crudely modular products (①) was supplanted by the integral dominant design, the Model T (②), and subsequent process innovations (the Ford System) and volume expansions (③). The GM System, which followed the Ford System, had a more closed-modular (e.g., common components) approach (④). The pace of product-process innovations then slowed down (Abernathy, 1978), but it has been increasing again since the 1970s, as global competition and environmental constraints have grown stronger (⑤ in advanced markets). This pattern of shifting frontiers roughly illustrates the architectural sequence and the long tail of the auto industry life cycle.

The automotive market was initially dominated by rich and function-oriented customers, followed by the price-oriented masses that Ford's Model T served. Since the 1970s, however, the function orientation has been regaining ground, due to both energy/safety/environmental constraints and customer sophistication. In addition, since the 2000s, the number of price-oriented customers at the lower end of emerging markets has rapidly increased (⑥). Concerning such low-end markets, note however that even the low-cost vehicles developed for them can be architecturally more integral when requirements for the products' functionality and integrity are relatively high (Lim & Fujimoto, 2019). In any case, their demands have been satisfied for the most part by simplified versions brought to market by existing auto manufacturers, rather than by disruptive technologies developed by new entrants (Christensen, 1997). Whether the integral segment in advanced markets and the modular segment in emerging ones (e.g., China) ultimately merge or remain separate will depend upon the extent to which the average requirements and constraints of the two markets converge, and at what level.

Still referring to Figure 23, the architectural sequence of the computer industry can be roughly described as follows: (①) emergence of seminal and integral computers ⇒ (②) dominant design with closed-modular architecture (System/360) ⇒ (③) drastic cost reductions, thanks to open-modular architecture (today's computers). The difference between the two patterns can be partially explained by the simple physical fact that passenger cars are weighty, fast and expensive consumer durables, while computers are operated by electrons and digital logic, which are essentially weightless and thus less constrained by safety/environment/energy concerns compared with the automobile.

7.4 Conclusions

This section sketched how the industry life cycle model can illuminate the early history of automotive product-process innovations but fails to explain the tail of the life cycle after the 1970s, whereas an evolutionary capability-architecture approach can complementarily describe the architectural sequence and the existence of the long tail of the automobile life cycle.

Over the past two decades, academic discussions around product innovations have been heavily focused on the area of digital products – and for good reason, considering the huge impact that digital technologies, with open architectures, platforms and ecosystems, have had on the global economy (Baldwin & Clark, 2000; Gawer & Cusumano, 2002; Iansiti & Levien, 2004). In the same period, however, a number of incidents have reminded us that we do, after all, live in the physical world, surrounded by a mixture of both the weighty and the weightless, analog and digital, real and virtual artifacts.

In order to successfully examine the industries of this century, as well as the future of automobiles, we must continue to investigate the design attributes of our artifacts, including their architectures and technologies, and the organizational attributes of design-production sites, including their manufacturing capabilities. Based on the historical-evolutionary analysis and capability-architecture view of the industry proposed in this Element so far, the author will continue to discuss the future of this complex industry.

8 Summary and Future

This compact Element on the evolution of the world automobile industry has explored its long-term dynamics regarding competitive performance (Section 2), product technology (Section 3), product architecture (Section 4), flows of value-carrying design information (Section 5), manufacturing capability (Section 6), and industry life cycle (Section 7).

This Element is not only an analysis of the automobile industry specifically but also an application of a more generic framework (see Section 1) that can be used to explain the evolution of any other industry, including machinery, digital, chemical, software, construction and services (Fujimoto & Ikuine, 2018). As such, it focuses on two main constructs that may significantly influence the dynamics of industrial performance, that is, organizational capability of industrial sites (genba) and product-process architecture. We may call this general approach to analyzing an industry's evolution the capability-architecture-performance (CAP) framework.

The next task is to investigate the future prospects of this industry/product in light of the CAP framework. In fact, the author has already completed the first draft of a manuscript on the automobile industry in the 2020s and beyond, but the space limitations of this Element do not allow for its inclusion here. Anyone interested in the matter may thus find further considerations around the future of the automobile industry in the author's forthcoming works (single-authored or coauthored with my research colleagues, such as John Paul MacDuffie). In this sense, the present Element can be regarded as the foundation for such future-oriented analyses, which are increasingly needed as this gigantic global industry faces a long-term transformation toward a safer and more sustainable, digital, serviceable and entertaining future.

References

Abernathy, W. J. (1978). *The Productivity Dilemma*, Baltimore: Johns Hopkins University Press.

Abernathy, W. J. & Utterback, J. M. (1978). Patterns of Industrial Innovation. *Technology Review*, **80**(7), 40–47.

Abernathy, W. J., Clark, K. B. & Kantrow, A. M. (1983). *Industrial Renaissance: Producing a Competitive Future for America*, New York: Basic Books.

Asanuma, B. (1989). Manufacturer-Supplier Relationships in Japan and the Concept of Relation-Specific Skill. *Journal of the Japanese and International Economies*, **3**, 1–30.

Baldwin, C. Y. & Clark, K. B. (2000). *Design Rules. Volume 1: The Power of Modularity*, Cambridge, MA: MIT Press.

Chandler, A. D. Jr. (1962). *Strategy and Structure*, Cambridge, MA: MIT Press.

Christensen, C. M. (1997). *The Innovator's Dilemma: When New Technologies Cause Great Firms to Fail*, Boston, MA: Harvard Business School Press.

Clark, K. B. (1985). The Interaction of Design Hierarchies and Market Concepts in Technological Evolution. *Research Policy*, 14, 235–251.

Clark, K. B. & Fujimoto, T. (1990). The Power of Product Integrity. *Harvard Business Review*, **68**(6), 107–118.

Clark, K. B. & Fujimoto, T. (1991). *Product Development Performance*, Boston, MA: Harvard Business School Press.

Cusumano, M. A. (1985). *The Japanese Automobile Industry: Technology and Management at Nissan and Toyota*, Cambridge, MA: Harvard University Press.

Cusumano, M. A. & Nobeoka, K. (1998). *Thinking Beyond Lean: How Multi-Project Management Is Transforming Product Development at Toyota and Other Companies*, New York: Free Press.

Fine, C. H. (1998). *Clockspeed: Winning Industry Control in the Age of Temporary Advantage*, Reading: Perseus Books.

Ford-Werke AG (1980). Mimeo, Herausforderung aus Osteuropa und Japan (in German).

Freeman, C. (1982). *The Economics of Industrial Innovation*, 2nd ed., Cambridge, MA: MIT Press.

Fujimoto, T. (1989). Organizations for Effective Product Development: The Case of the Global Automobile Industry, unpublished DBA. Dissertation, Harvard Business School.

Fujimoto, T. (1999). *The Evolution of a Manufacturing System at Toyota*, New York: Oxford University Press.

Fujimoto T. (2001). The Japanese Automobile Parts Supplier System: The Triplet of Effective Inter-Firm Routines. *International Journal of Automotive Technology and Management*, 1(1), 1–34.

Fujimoto, T. (2007a). Architecture-Based Comparative Advantage: A Design Information View of Manufacturing. *Evolutionary and Institutional Economics Review*, 4(1), 55–112.

Fujimoto, T. (2007b). *Competing to be Really, Really Good: The Behind-the-Scenes Drama of Capability-Building Competition in the Automobile Industry*, LTCB International Library Trust, Tokyo: International House of Japan.

Fujimoto, T. (2012). An Economic Analysis of Architecture and Coordination: Applying Ricardian Comparative Advantage to Design Costs and Locations. *Evolutionary and Institutional Economics Review*, 9(1), 51–124.

Fujimoto, T. (2014). The Long Tail of the Auto Industry Life Cycle. *The Journal of Product Innovation Management*, 31(1), 8–16.

Fujimoto, T. & Heller D. A., eds. (2018). *Industries and Disasters: Building Robust and Competitive Supply Chains*, New York: Nova Science.

Fujimoto, T. & Ikuine, F., eds. (2018). *Industrial Competitiveness and Design Evolution*, Tokyo: Springer.

Fujimoto, T. & Raff, D. (1999). Conclusion. In Y. Lung, J. Chanaron, T. Fujimoto & D. Raff, eds., *Coping with Variety*, Hampshire: Ashgate.

Fujimoto, T. & Shiozawa, Y. (2011–2012). Inter and Intra Company Competition in the Age of Global Competition: A Micro and Macro Interpretation of Ricardian Trade Theory. *Evolutionary and Institutional Economics Review*, 8(2), 193–231.

Gawer, A. & Cusumano, M. A. (2002). *Platform Leadership: How Intel, Microsoft, and Cisco Drive Industry Innovation*, Boston, MA: Harvard Business School Press.

Grant, R. M. (1991). The Resource-Based Theory of Competitive Advantage: Implications for Strategy Formulation. *California Management Review*, 33 (3), 114–135.

Grant, R. M. (2016). *Contemporary Strategy Analysis*, 9th ed., Hoboken, NJ: Wiley.

Heller, D. A., Mercer, G. & Fujimoto, T. (2006). The Long-Term Value of M&A Activity That Enhances Learning Organizations. *International Journal of Automotive Technology and Management*, 6(2), 157–176.

Helper, S. & Sako, M. (1995). Supplier Relations in Japan and the United States: Are They Converging? *Sloan Management Review*, 36(3), 77–84.

Holweg, M. & Pil, F. K. (2004). *The Second Century: Reconnecting Customer and Value Chain through Build-to-Order: Moving beyond Mass and Lean Production in the Auto Industry*, Cambridge, MA: MIT Press.

Hounshell, D. A. (1984). *From the American System to Mass Production, 1800–1932: The Development of Manufacturing Technology in the United States*, Baltimore: Johns Hopkins University Press.

Iansiti, M. & Levien, R. (2004). *The Keystone Advantage: What the New Dynamics of Business Ecosystems Mean for Strategy, Innovation, and Sustainability*, Boston: Harvard Business School Press.

Imai, M. (1986). *Kaizen (Ky'zen): The Key to Japan's Competitive Success*, 1st ed., New York: Random House Business Division.

Lancaster, K. J. (1966). A New Approach to Consumer Theory. *Journal of Political Economy*, **74**(2), 132–157.

Liker, J. K. (2004). *The Toyota Way: 14 Management Principles from the World's Greatest Manufacturer*, New York: McGraw Hill.

Liker, J. K. & Ross, K. (2017). *The Toyota Way to Service Excellence*, New York: McGraw Hill.

Lim, C. & Fujimoto, T. (2019). Frugal Innovation and Design Changes Expanding the Cost-Performance Frontier: A Schumpeterian Approach. *Research Policy*, **48**(4), 1016–1029.

MacDuffie, J. P. & Fujimoto, T. (2010). Why Dinosaurs Will Keep Ruling the Auto Industry. *Harvard Business Review*, **88**(6), 23–25.

Maxcy, G. & Silberston, A. (1959). *The Motor Industry*, London: Allen & Unwin.

Mintzberg, H. & Waters, J. A. (1985). Of Strategies, Deliberate and Emergent. *Strategic Management Journal*, **6**(3), 257–272.

Monden, Y. (1983). *Toyota Production System: Practical Approach to Production Management*, Norcross, GA: Industrial Engineering and Management Press.

Nelson, R. R. & Winter, S. G. (1982). *An Evolutionary Theory of Economic Change*, Cambridge, MA: Harvard University Press.

Nishiguchi, T. (1994). *Strategic Industrial Sourcing*, Oxford: Oxford University Press.

Ohno, T. (1978). *Toyota Seisan Hoshiki (Toyota Production System)*, (in Japanese), Tokyo: Daiyamondo-sha.

Penrose, E. T. (1959). *The Theory of the Growth of the Firm*, Oxford: Basil Blackwell.

Schonberger, R. (1982). *Japanese Manufacturing Techniques: Nine Hidden Lessons in Simplicity*, New York: Free Press.

Shimokawa, K., Jurgens, U. & Fujimoto, T., eds. (1997). *Transforming Automobile Assembly: Experience in Automation and Work Organization*, Berlin: Springer.

Shingo, S. (1981). *A Study of the Toyota Production System from an Industrial Engineering Viewpoint*, Tokyo: Japan Management Association.

Simon, H. A. (1969). *The Science of the Artificial*, Cambridge, MA: MIT Press.

Spender, J.-C. (2014). *Business Strategy: Managing Uncertainty, Opportunity, & Enterprise*, Oxford: Oxford University Press.

Suh, N. P. (1990). *The Principles of Design*, New York: Oxford University Press.

Teece, D. J. (2007). Explicating Dynamic Capabilities: The Nature and Microfoundations of (Sustainable) Enterprise Performance. *Strategic Management Journal*, **28**, 1319–1350.

Teece, D. J. & Pisano, G. (1994). The Dynamic Capabilities of Firms: An Introduction. *Industrial and Corporate Change*, **3**(3), 537–556.

Thomke, S. & Fujimoto, T. (2000). The Effect of "Front-Loading" Problem-Solving on Product Development Performance. *Journal of Product Innovation Management*, **17**(2), 128–142.

Uchida, T. (2017). *Virtual Engineering*. Nikkan Kogyo Shinbunsha (in Japanese).

Ulrich, K. T. (1995). The Role of Product Architecture in the Manufacturing Firm. *Research Policy*, **24**(3), 419–440.

Womack, J. P. & Jones, D. T. (1996). Lean Thinking: Banish Waste and Create Wealth in Your Corporation, New York: Simon & Schuster.

Womack, J. P., Jones, D. T. & Roos, D. (1990). *The Machine That Changed the World*, New York: Rawson Associates.

Acknowledgment

The first suggestion to write this Element on the Japanese automobile industry came in December 2015 from Professor J.-C. Spender, whom I have known for years as a respected scholar of strategic management. I had already published lengthier volumes in English on product development in the automobile industry (Clark & Fujimoto, 1991), Toyota-style manufacturing systems (Fujimoto, 1999), and the Japanese automobile industry (Fujimoto, 2007b), so I thought that it would not be difficult to write another text, not only on the Japanese case but on the world automobile industry at large.

Yet, this Element writing project turned out to be a difficult one to finish. Indeed, in the late 2010s, a wave of digital transformations seemed to sweep over the automobile industry. Most people in popular journalism claimed that disruptive innovations and industry revolutions would completely transform the structure of the world auto industry, including crises of incumbent automakers. Countless new articles and reports were published on automobile-related digital technologies, mobility business platforms, trials of autonomous driving, new architecture of embedded software, advanced EVs, entries of infotainment players, and so on.

On the other hand, however, through many years of empirical and theoretical academic research on this industry, I have come to believe that one aspect will remain fundamentally unchanged, that is, the simple fact that the car is a heavy and complex physical object used in public spaces (roads), which is therefore severely constrained by physical laws, as well as energy, environmental and safety regulations. The passenger car, owned or shared, will also continue to be an attractive means of long-haul personal mobility for many people worldwide.

I would like to thank numerous academic and industrial experts who, for many years, have provided me with precious information and insights into the dynamics of this industry. I would also like to express my sincere gratitude to Professor Spender for his patience and support to this awfully delayed project and to Ms. Francesca Viarengo, who has continually conducted excellent proofreading work and offered valuable comments as the very first reader of several of my books/papers, including this one. Last but not least, my thanks go to the staff of the Manufacturing Management Research Center (MMRC) at the University of Tokyo and the Monozukuri Kaizen Network (MKN), who have given me logistic and financial support for this project, as well as Professor John Paul MacDuffie of the Wharton School, University of Pennsylvania, Director of the International Motor Vehicle Program (IMVP) and Program on Vehicle and

Mobility Innovation (PVMI), and Dr. Tammaso Pardi of École normale supérieure de Paris-Saclay, Director of GERPISA – Le Réseau International de L'Automobile, for kindly providing this Element with very constructive reviews.

August 2020 and April 2023, at home in Tokyo and in a small mountain cottage in Nagano, Japan Takahiro Fujimoto

Cambridge Elements ☰

Business Strategy

J.-C. Spender
Kozminski University

J.-C. Spender is a research professor, Kozminski University. He has been active in the business strategy field since 1971 and is the author or coauthor of seven books and numerous papers. His principal academic interest is in knowledge-based theories of the private sector firm, and managing them.

Advisory Board

About the Series

Business strategy's reach is vast, and important too since wherever there is business activity there is strategizing. As a field, strategy has a long history from medieval and colonial times to today's developed and developing economies. This series offers a place for interesting and illuminating research including industry and corporate studies, strategizing in service industries, the arts, the public sector, and the new forms of Internet-based commerce. It also covers today's expanding gamut of analytic techniques.

Cambridge Elements $^{\equiv}$

Business Strategy

Printed in the United States
by Baker & Taylor Publisher Services